Praise for *Run to Win*

"Vince Lombardi was a master in knowing how to take a group of diverse people and turn them into a winning team. The principles he employed are identical to those that help grow a successful business. This is a book I'll keep handy."

—Rosalind Cole, president, Personalities
and Promotions International

"My father had the greatest respect for Vince Lombardi, the man, the friend, the legend, the leader. *Run to Win* captures the essence of who Mr. Lombardi was like no book I've ever read. It is simply compelling. Now everyone will understand why my father named the Super Bowl Trophy after him."

—Anne Marie Rozelle Bratton, Pete Rozelle's daughter,
and independent businesswoman

"*Run to Win* is one of the most inspiring books I've ever read. With lucid and compelling prose, Don Phillips has illuminated Vince Lombardi's leadership ability in a most extraordinary way. Every athletic coach in the nation should own a copy of this book."

—Grant Teaff, executive director of the 10,000 member
American Football Coaches Association

Also by Donald T. Phillips

Lincoln on Leadership: Executive Strategies for Tough Times

On the Brink: The Life and Leadership of Norman Brinker
(with Norman Brinker)

Lincoln Stories for Leaders

The Founding Fathers on Leadership:
Classic Teamwork in Changing Times

Martin Luther King, Jr. on Leadership:
Inspiration & Wisdom for Challenging Times

A Diamond in Spring

Leading with the Heart: Coach K's Successful Strategies
for Basketball, Business, and Life
(with Mike Krzyzewski)

RUN TO WIN

VINCE LOMBARDI
On Coaching and Leadership

Donald T. Phillips

ST. MARTIN'S GRIFFIN
NEW YORK

www.stmartins.com

Library of Congress Cataloging-in-Publication Data

Phillips, Donald T.
    Run to win : Vince Lombardi on coaching and leadership / Donald T. Phillips.
        p. cm.
    Includes bibliographical references and index.
    ISBN 0-312-27298-7 (hc)
    ISBN 0-312-30308-4 (pbk)
    1. Lombardi, Vince. 2. Football coaches—United States—Biography.
  3. Leadership. I. Title: Vince Lombardi on coaching and leadership. II. Title.

GV939.L6 P45 2001
796.332'092—dc21   2001031950
[B]

10 9 8 7 6 5 4 3 2

*Dedicated to the members of the
American Football Coaches Association*

Brethren: Don't you know that while all the runners in the stadium take part in the race, only one wins the prize. Run to win.

ST. PAUL'S FIRST EPISTLE TO THE CORINTHIANS

I CORINTHIANS 9:24

(NEW AMERICAN BIBLE; CATHOLIC)

CONTENTS

INTRODUCTION   1

PART I | STARTING OUT

1   First Prepare   13

2   Build Your Team   18

3   Know Your Stuff   25

4   Develop a Game Plan   32

5   Encourage Innovation, Imagination, and Creativity   37

PART II | BUILDING TRUST

6   Sell Yourself   47

7   Treat People As Individuals   54

8   Be Color-blind   62

9   Keep Things Simple   67

10   Constantly Inspire and Motivate   72

PART III | ROUTINE

11   Take Charge   83

12   Learn, Teach, Practice   90

13   Focus on Physical Fitness, Discipline, and
     Mental Toughness   98

14   Run to Daylight   109

15   Have the Will to Win   116

PART IV | CHARACTER

16   Have the Courage to Lead   129

17   Control Your Darker Side   135

18   Preach Love, Family, and Heart Power   144

19   Be Willing to Pay the Price for Success   153

20   Make a Commitment to Excellence   160

EPILOGUE   174
ACKNOWLEDGMENTS   185
BIBLIOGRAPHY   187
INDEX   189

Okay, everybody, let's go.
VINCE LOMBARDI

We knew that the only difference between being a good football team and a great football team was him and only him.

JERRY KRAMER,
GUARD, GREEN BAY PACKERS,
ON VINCE LOMBARDI

INTRODUCTION

"Vincent Lombardi!?" exclaimed a member of the executive board of the Green Bay Packers. "Who the hell is Vincent Lombardi?"

It was January 1959, and the Packers' selection committee had just announced the individual they had chosen to be the team's new head coach and general manager. When that decision was subsequently announced to the public, nearly every football fan in Wisconsin was asking precisely the same question—"Who the hell is Vince Lombardi?"

The committee not only had picked a virtual unknown to run the team; they had chosen an "old man" who had never before led an NFL team, never even been a college head coach. As a matter of fact, the last head coaching job he had held was at a high school in New Jersey, and that was more than a decade ago. *A forty-five-year-old rookie head coach!* thought many Packer fans. *Who are they kidding?*

But this was no joking matter to the "old man" who had worked long and hard to finally be given the chance to lead a professional football team. He had snapped up the Packer offer without hesitation and intended to make good on the opportunity. For him, the time was right. His whole life had been in preparation for this job.

| | |

Vincent Thomas Lombardi was born in Brooklyn, New York, on June 11, 1913. The eldest of five children, he was heavily influenced by the contrasting personalities of a doting mother and a domineering father. His mother, Matilda, soft, kind, and caring, provided a strong religious-oriented, stable Catholic household. His father, Harry, came over on the boat from Italy. At the age of eleven, he quit school to help support his family and became a well-respected and successful butcher. Short, stocky, and strong, Vince's father was hot-tempered and overbearing. He had an intimidating style about him that allowed no back talk from his children. But he was also honest, straightforward, and a pure perfectionist. Those around him had to do things right or not at all. He constantly lectured his three sons that they'd be successful only if they worked harder than everybody else. "We got no weekly allowance and you had to earn your money with him," Vince recalled. In addition, Harry always advised his sons on how to succeed in life. "Before you can do what you want to do," he told them, "before you can exist as an individual, the first thing you have to accept is duty, the second thing is respect for authority, and the third . . . is to develop a strong mental discipline."

While growing up, Vince participated in many sports. He played basketball, baseball, even fought and won a Golden Gloves boxing match. But football was his real love. During his senior year in high school, he won a scholarship to St. Francis Prep School in Brooklyn. The coach there, Harry Kane, drilled the players on fundamentals and learning by repetition. "It was so many steps out and over and then in," remembered Vince, "and he made the reasons clear."

After Lombardi made the All-City team as a fullback, he applied for and gained admittance to Fordham University, where he earned a spot on the football team. In 1932, Fordham was the largest Catholic university in the nation—famous for stressing character building and the development of social morality. The school's head football coach, Jim Crowley, was a protégé of legendary coach Knute Rockne—and one of the famous "Four Horsemen" of Notre Dame University's offensive backfield.

Crowley had an enormous impact on the young Lombardi. During practice sessions, he advocated "no loafing, no halfhearted effort, no indifference either mental or physical, but hard, aggressive, brainy work from beginning to end." Coach Crowley was also a great orator in the tradition of Rockne. During Vince's senior year, in 1936, for example, Crowley gave a now-famous pregame pep talk in which he concluded by turning to the student manager and warning: "Son, you better open that door and get out of the way fast! Here comes my Fordham team!"

Vince developed a close relationship with Crowley's assistant coach, Frank Leahy, who went on to become a great head coach in his own right with Notre Dame and Boston College. Leahy spent a lot of time working one-on-one with members of the offensive line, which, of course, included Vince. At an early practice, Leahy ordered Lombardi to block him personally. When the two crouched down into a three-point stance, Leahy quickly launched into Vince and knocked him on his can. "Let's do it again," demanded Leahy. This time, however, Vince quickly charged his coach and reeled *him* backward. "Okay, Vinnie," said Leahy upon picking himself up, "you pass."

Crowley took note of Vince's size and toughness and immediately moved him from fullback to guard on the offensive line. "He wasn't fast enough" for fullback, said the coach. However, friends pointed out, Vince was a "rugged character" with "inspiration" who "hardly ever made a mistake" and "didn't like to lose." "He didn't shine," recalled Crowley, "but he was a good, steady player and always reliable, responsible, and very dependable."

Lombardi took a good deal of ribbing from his teammates when he was moved to guard—a position they described as "a fullback with his brains knocked out." But Vince overcame the ridicule by working so long and so hard Leahy made him a starting member of Fordham's "Seven Blocks of Granite," one of the most famous offensive front lines in college football history.

At Fordham, Lombardi quickly gained a reputation for being extremely tough—playing all-out, even when seriously hurt. At one practice, after suffering a separation of his small intestine, he was carried off the field writhing in pain. Severe internal bleeding landed him in the hospital. But, amazingly, he showed up for practice the next day, only to collapse on the sidelines. So, again, the trainers hauled him back to the hospital, where he was confined for several more days.

On another occasion, Lombardi continued to play a regular-season game even though several of his teeth had been knocked out. "We had a play on which I was supposed to trap the Pitt tackle," Vince recollected. "It worked fine, so our quarterback kept calling it. But every time I trapped that guy, he jabbed me right in the teeth with his elbow." A friend noted that Vince played the rest of the game "with blood gushing from his mouth." In later years, Lombardi was fond of retelling the story—saying that his father had often told him to ignore the small injuries, that "hurt is in the mind." "When I got home that night," he would joke, "I was certainly hurting in my mind."

After graduation from Fordham, Vince wandered for a time. He played semipro ball with small franchises in Wilmington, Delaware, and Springfield, Massachusetts, and later had a short stint with the Brooklyn Eagles of the American Football Association. He also spent a semester at Fordham Law School, was a chemist for DuPont Chemical Company, and attempted to enlist in the army but was rejected because of poor eyesight. He took a job as an assistant manager at a finance company but quit because he didn't like the work—especially when it involved pressuring poor people to pay up on their loans. He was also so kindhearted that he often ended up giving people money out of his own pocket to help them make their payments.

Because he wanted to work with young people and also because he wanted to marry his girlfriend, Marie Planitz, Vince finally accepted a full-time job at St. Cecilia High School in Englewood, New Jersey—and he stayed there for the next eight years, teaching chemistry, physics, biology, Latin, and physical education. Former students described his teaching style as stern and disciplined. They remembered that they "could hear a pin drop in his class" as he walked "around that room like a tiger," barking out his lectures in a "low, booming voice."

At St. Cecilia, Vince was also given his first opportunity to coach both football and basketball—and he turned out to be extraordinarily successful at both. Under his direction, the high school won six state championships in the two sports. In football, Lombardi's teams ran off a thirty-two-game unbeaten streak. And, at one point, his basketball teams won twenty-three games in a row. One local sportswriter took particular note of the winning ways at St. Cecilia and gave much credit to the school's head coach. "Vincent Lombardi is an unusual young man," wrote the journalist. "He is a hard taskmaster yet is sincerely admired and respected by all of his charges. He demands perfection and gets it because his boys are willing to work for and with him." Part of the reason that Lombardi's players were willing to work with him was that he nurtured and cared for them like a father. When Lombardi succeeded, so did they. As a matter of fact, twenty-two of St. Cecilia's players were named to All-County and All-State teams while he was coach.

In 1947, Lombardi accepted a job offer at his alma mater, Fordham University, as assistant football coach and assistant director of physical education. And after two years of primarily leading the freshman football team, he was asked to interview for an assistant coaching position at the United States Military Academy at West Point, New York. Vince knew that this would be a wonderful chance to work with legendary coach Earl "Red" Blaik, who had led Army teams to several undefeated seasons and a national championship. Blaik, a former Army colonel, was also famous for having trained a multitude of individuals who had gone on to head coaching jobs at other prestigious colleges around the nation.

So it was no surprise that when the West Point sports information director called Vince to offer him the job, Lombardi screamed, "I'll take it!" into the phone before the director even had the chance to make the offer.

Over the next five years, the two men spent a great deal of time together as Vince latched onto the colonel as a teacher and mentor. And Blaik remembered being immediately impressed with his new protégé. "I saw the sparkle in his eyes," said the veteran coach of Vince Lombardi, "[and] I knew he was ready." They watched thousands of hours of game films together. They studied offenses, defenses; debated and devised strategies; and discussed the similarities of their sport to life. With time, as Vince learned and grew, he became more and more confident as a coach and a leader of men. Eventually, he began offering his own new ideas and daring innovations, many of which were implemented.

Coach Earl Blaik was an important person for Vince Lombardi to have adopted as a mentor. His practice sessions were precise, efficient, and highly organized. He was meticulous in his understanding and teaching of the sport—and very demanding in its execution by the players. And Earl Blaik was conscientious, honest, and fair, though also a hardworking, stern taskmaster. He was a man who didn't take vacations, who was determined, persistent, and driven to succeed. "You have to pay the price," Blaik constantly lectured his players. "You have to pay the price for success."

Vince savored every moment and appreciated all that he had learned from his mentor. In later years a grateful Lombardi said of Blaik: "He worked on me and molded me and fashioned my entire approach to the game. . . . I cannot conceive of a greater coach than Red Blaik."

The New York Giants of the National Football League must have thought exactly the same thing. Because after suffering through the worst season in their history in 1953 (with a dismal 3–12 record), the Giants fired their head coach and offered the job to Blaik. But despite repeated wining, dining, and high-dollar offers, the colonel decided to remain at West Point. He did give permission, however, for the Giants to speak with Vince Lombardi about a position as assistant coach. It turned out that Lombardi's longtime friend and former classmate at Fordham, Wellington Mara, was now an executive for the Giants. Actually, his family owned the franchise. So, with a significant connection and with a substantial increase in salary, Vince left the ranks of college football and went to work for the high-profile New York Giants.

Interestingly enough, Jim Lee Howell, the new head coach of the Giants, was, at age thirty-nine, two years younger than Vince. Howell had a "hands-off" style that allowed his assistant coaches a wide latitude and a significant amount of authority to do as they pleased with their charges. So while Howell sat back and handled the media, football field operations were run by two men who he bragged were "the two smartest assistant coaches in football": Vince Lombardi on offense and Tom Landry on defense.

Both Landry and Lombardi approached their jobs with a fierce intensity and driving competitiveness. They studied game films, spent time getting to know the players, and worked hard at forging a winning attitude on what had been a losing team. One player, Kyle Rote, later described a normal scene each morning at the New York Giants training office: "I'd look to the left and see Lombardi in a room running the projector for his plays and I'd look to the right and I'd see Landry running *his* plays, and then on down the hall I'd look in Jim's Lee's room and see him reading the newspaper."

"The Giants didn't have a head coach," quipped one New York sportswriter. "They had a head smile."

But Howell's "smile" strategy worked. The Giants forged winning seasons in the first two years of the Lombardi-Landry tandem. And then they became champions of the National Football League by smashing the Chicago Bears 47–7 in the title game of 1956.

The success of the New York Giants eventually catapulted both men into head coaching roles of their own. The last game Landry and Lombardi coached together is considered by many the greatest game in NFL history—the 1958 championship against the Johnny Unitas–led Baltimore Colts. The Giants lost in overtime. Tom Landry left in 1960 to coach the Dallas Cowboys for twenty-nine consecutive years—and Vince Lombardi, of course, had moved on to lead the Packers one year earlier (1959).

Before Lombardi showed up in Green Bay, the Packer team had experienced eleven consecutive losing seasons. While he was there, they had nine winning seasons in a row—which included six Western Conference titles, five NFL titles (three of them in a row), and victories in the first two Super Bowls.

During Lombardi's ten seasons as a head football coach in the NFL, he lost only one postseason game—the first one. Then he ran off nine play-off victories in a row. But the year after he stepped down as head coach at Green Bay, the Packers finished 6–7 and did not make the play-offs. During his one year with the Washington Redskins, the team finished 7–5 after having suffered through fourteen consecutive losing seasons.

By the end of his career, it had become clear to everyone that Vince Lombardi's presence on a football team made the difference between winning and losing—and that he was one great football coach, one great leader of men. Jerry Kramer, a guard for the Packers, may have summed it up best when he said simply: "We knew that the only difference between being a good football team and a great football team was him and only him."

Vince Lombardi coached during a time of significant transition for professional football. He was one of the first successful professional coaches to be subjected to large televised press conferences. CBS began airing NFL games nationally on TV during Vince's second year with the Giants (1955). And *Sports Illustrated*'s weekly coverage of professional football started shortly thereafter. By the time Lombardi got to Green Bay, the average attendance at NFL games had increased by 60 percent, individual team revenues were beginning to swell, and television audiences were growing exponentially. Nine years later, more than 70 million people watched his last game with the Packers in Super Bowl II.

At Vince Lombardi's very first game in Green Bay, people observed a not-very-impressive-looking "old man" in a rumpled raincoat standing on the sidelines—and they wondered who the hell he was and where he had come from. But a decade later, when he left, he was one of the most famous people in the nation. During that time, Lombardi set standards others only dream of achieving. His .758 winning percentage is one of the highest in the history of the National Football League. And in all of his years as a head football coach, he never had a losing season, nor even a .500 season. Vince Lombardi had only winning seasons.

His coaching style and his personality have been written about, talked about, and debated. Schools, streets, arenas, and medical centers are named in his honor. When college football selects its best defensive lineman, they give that player the Lombardi Award. He's also enshrined in the National Football League's Hall of Fame—and when an NFL team wins the Super Bowl, they are awarded the silver-plated Lombardi Trophy.

There is today something of a mystique about Vince Lombardi. At times, the legend and the myth seem to have grown beyond the man. But Vince Lombardi was, indeed, just a man—a very complex, emotional, compassionate, hard-driven man.

And if he were still with us, if someone were to ask him about his philosophy on coaching, on leadership, or on life in general, what would he tell us?

Well, as Lombardi himself probably would have phrased it . . .

"Listen up, mister. I've got something to say."

On September 27, 1959, a sellout crowd packed Green Bay, Wisconsin's Lambeau Field for the first game of the regular season against their team's powerful arch rival, the "hated" Chicago Bears. The previous season, Green Bay's beloved Packers had finished last in the National Football League with a pitiful 1-10-1 record. Still, the fans had hope. There was anticipation and excitement in the air. It was the beginning of a new season, and anything could happen.

The game started out well as the Packers recovered a Bears fumble on the opening kickoff. And then, on their first offensive play, something unusual happened. Packer halfback Paul Hornung took a handoff from the quarterback, ran to his left, and then threw the ball downfield to a wide open receiver running near the goal line.

The crowd jumped to their feet in amazement. This was new! This was different! Wow!

But Lew Carpenter dropped the ball. And when the Packers subsequently missed a short field goal attempt, the crowd settled back in a disappointment that things might not be so new and different after all.

At halftime, the heavily favored Bears had a meager 3–0 lead. And in the Packers locker room, the team's new head coach praised his players for their first-half output, for their determination, for their commitment to making an outstanding effort.

"And now, men of Green Bay, step aside," said the coach, closing out his pep talk. "Make way for the mightiest Green Bay team in years! A winning team! Go get 'em, Green Bay!" In response, an emotionally charged Packer team slammed their arms against lockers, screamed in determination, ran out of the locker room, and stormed onto the field.

For the remainder of the game, the Green Bay defense held Chicago to a lonely fourth-quarter field goal. Then, trailing 6–0, the Packer offense finally broke through for a touchdown to take the lead by a single point. The hometown crowd launched into a delirious frenzy, which served to further fire up the Packer players. A few minutes later, the team's defensive line produced two points of their own by tackling a Bears runner in the end zone for a safety.

When the final gun sounded and Green Bay had beaten Chicago by a score of 9–6, the Packer players hoisted the head coach to their shoulders and ran off the field with him in triumph.

"We're on our way now!" shouted an emotional Vince Lombardi at the top of his lungs.

PART I
Starting Out

You have to start somewhere. When you start to coach, you coach the system you played, but you begin almost immediately to discard what doesn't fit you or your material, and you look for what does.

VINCE LOMBARDI

I've been up here all year and I've learned a lot. I know how the towns-people are and what they think of you men.

VINCE LOMBARDI,
AT HIS FIRST TEAM MEETING WITH THE GREEN BAY PACKERS

When I came to Green Bay in 1959, before we went to training camp we ran and reran the films of all the Packers' games of the previous two years. We graded every player and then we sat down to see what our primary needs were.

VINCE LOMBARDI

1   *First Prepare*

The Green Bay Packers had a proud history. They were one of the thirteen original franchises in the National Football League's first season of 1921. And they were the only small-town team to survive the Great Depression of the 1930s. Founded and coached by Earl "Curly" Lambeau, who played at Notre Dame under Knute Rockne, the early Packers were known for their successful implementation of the forward pass—and for their winning ways.

But after World War II the team fell on hard times. And by 1958 they had become an NFL joke. The Packers were a laughingstock, acknowledged as the worst team in the league. NFL players referred to Green Bay as "Siberia" and feared being traded there. College seniors prayed they wouldn't be drafted by the Packers.

The hometown fans hadn't seen so much as a .500 season since 1947 and were consistently embarrassed by the team's shoddy performances. It seemed as though every person in Wisconsin was complaining about the Packers. In the club, itself, there was an overwhelming air of defeatism. Many players dressed sloppily, showed up late to practice, were always griping and mouthing off. Some had little respect for authority and actually took themselves out of games and put themselves back in whenever they felt like it. In 1958, the team finished 1-10-1. It was their eleventh straight losing season. And the entire year had been capped by a humiliating 56–0 home loss to the Baltimore Colts—a disaster that was televised throughout the Midwest.

It was at this point that management fired their head coach and began to take a serious look at Vince Lombardi. Red Blaik gave his former protégé a great recommendation, as did Paul Brown of the Cleveland Browns. Even George Halas, of the rival Chicago Bears, said: "He'll be a good one." Wellington Mara at first balked and then relented at the thought of his friend leaving the Giants. But Mara knew Vince was ready and would be a great head coach—and told the Packers as much. So the executive board gave the nod to Lombardi but, in so doing, offered him one of the lowest salaries for a head coach in the entire league. Vince, however, graciously accepted the offer. He realized that since the team wasn't winning, they weren't making any money, either. The board, though, also compensated Lombardi by making him general manager. If the team did well, he also would do well. It was a good arrangement, because he'd have complete say over how he built and ran the team. And so forty-five-year-old Vince Lombardi—the Packers' fourth head coach in nine years—took over the team for the 1959 season.

Immediately after formally accepting the job, Vince drove to his church and spent much of the day praying. The next morning he flew to Green Bay and met with members of the executive board, with whom he discussed his vision for the team. Then Lombardi conducted his first briefing with members of the Wisconsin press—but he cautioned them. "I'm no miracle worker," he said humbly.

In preparing to coach the Green Bay Packers back to respectability, Lombardi began quietly. Not only did he look within himself and pray for spiritual guidance; he set about carefully studying the team he had just inherited.

Before meeting with any of the players, he closely scrutinized films of previous Packer games. As a matter of fact, during his first three months as coach, Lombardi reviewed more than twenty thousand feet of film. "From morning until night and week after week," he said, ". . . we ran and reran the films of all the Packers' games of the previous two years."

This was the very same method of preparation he had learned at West Point from Coach Red Blaik—who later recalled that he and Vince had watched game films until "our brain lobes felt as worn as the film sprocket holes looked." Lombardi had also used the technique when he first became an assistant coach with the New York Giants. Back then, he hung a sheet up in the den of his house, set up a projector, and watched film of the Giants' offense all day and all night until, as he said, "it began to drive Marie and the kids crazy, and I had to take it down to the basement." And he would do the same thing many years later in his career after accepting a job with the Washington Redskins—whose players were so ill-prepared that they were "always making up plays in the huddle."

Lombardi's actions when studying the game films were both industrious and meticulous. He not only wanted to study each player; he also wanted to familiarize himself with every defense and offense on his team and in the league. "On each play in every game I'd run the projector back and forth three or four times with seven or eight people in mind," he once wrote, "and then I'd run it back again to see what the three or four others were doing."

He also took extensive notes and, on yellow writing pads, charted each play for both offense and defense. Then he organized everything into an orderly and easily accessible filing system. Next, Lombardi graded every player, wrote a report on each of them, compared reports, and then made judgments as to whether each player should stay or go. "You have to start somewhere," Lombardi remarked of his meticulous study and preparation. "When you start to coach you coach the system you played, but you begin almost immediately to discard what doesn't fit you or your material, and you look for what does."

Once he learned everything he could possibly learn about his new team, Lombardi began to evaluate the situation in terms of strengths and weaknesses. He deduced that the Packers were strong in a few areas, notably at fullback, offensive end, tackle, center, and linebacker. But the weaknesses, he concluded, were almost overwhelming. As a matter of fact, Vince was beside himself when he realized that nearly the entire Packer defense was substandard. "We need help on both the defensive line and the defensive backfield," he lamented. On offense, he concluded that the guards were weak, the halfbacks were slow, and there was a "puzzle" at quarterback. "I think I have taken on more than I can handle," he told his secretary one day. "Will you pray for me and help me?"

Lombardi did note, however, that there were a couple of very strong players on the team—men who had a chance to be leaders on the squad and stars in their own right. On offense, he described Forrest Gregg as the "one professional on our team." Lombardi was also extremely impressed with running back Paul Hornung, who had been a quarterback at Notre Dame. When Vince saw how well Hornung could throw the ball, he naturally began to consider extensive use of the halfback option—just as he had done with a New York Giant running back named Frank Gifford.

In addition to immersing himself in the technical details of the football team, Lombardi began a personal marketing and public relations campaign. He traveled throughout Wisconsin promoting the team and hawking season ticket sales, which, quite understandably, had been extremely sluggish. He strategically sought to bring a sense of pride back to the Packers. So he called on public officials and industry executives in both Green Bay and Milwaukee and asked for their support.

And Lombardi made countless speeches on behalf of the team, addressing audiences both large and small. On one hand, he'd tell his listeners that "this is not a Green Bay football team but a Wisconsin team." On the other, he'd play on the Packers' small-town image as sentimental favorites: "It's the old David verses Goliath theme," he'd say. "They all want us to beat the big towns." And he'd try to fire up supporters by letting them know that he intended for the Green Bay Packers to be winners. "There is no substitute for victory!" exclaimed the forceful new head coach. "We shall play every game to the hilt with every ounce of fiber we have in our bodies."

After reviewing the films and barnstorming the state, Lombardi began meeting with the Packer players—one-on-one and in groups. He let them know that not only had he been evaluating their past individual performances, but he also had been listening to the fans. "I've been up here all year and I've learned a lot," he said. "I know how the townspeople are and what they think of you men."

And clearly, Vince had no doubts that he was going to succeed. To one veteran, he said privately (and wryly): "Just stay with me. I'm gonna build a dynasty here . . . heh, heh, heh."

Lombardi Principles

- When you're given a chance to coach, accept the offer graciously.
- Look within yourself and pray for spiritual guidance.
- Go meet with executives of the team and discuss your vision for the future.
- When you first meet with members of the press, be humble.
- Study in detail the team you've just inherited.
- Be both industrious and meticulous in your analysis. Take extensive notes. Organize and file.
- Discard what doesn't fit you or your material. Look for what does fit.
- Evaluate the situation in terms of existing strengths and weaknesses.
- Undertake a personal marketing and public relations campaign.
- Call on public officials and industry executives and ask for their support.
- Seek strategically to build a sense of pride in your team.

Our single most important public is our own employees—our team. For without a skilled, coordinated group of talented people behind us, we haven't a chance in the world of attaining success.

VINCE LOMBARDI

You were chosen to be a Green Bay Packer.

VINCE LOMBARDI,
TO HIS TEAM ON THE FIRST DAY OF PRACTICE

No! No! Together! Together! Not like a typewriter.

VINCE LOMBARDI,
TO THE PACKERS DURING DRILLS,
AS HE STOOD ON THE BACK OF THE BLOCKING SLED

2 Build Your Team

"I'm looking for a defensive backfield coach," Vince Lombardi said to thirty-one-year-old Norb Hecker.

"Well, I'm looking for a job," Hecker replied. "I played eight years of pro ball and did a little coaching up in Canada."

Over the course of the conversation, Lombardi did not seem at all concerned that the young man he was interviewing had almost no coaching experience. Rather, he inquired mostly about his family and personal background.

"He never asked me about my philosophy or theory of football," remembered Hecker. "He never put me at the blackboard. I found out later he'd gotten some good recommendations about me from coaches I'd played for."

"The job's yours if you want it," Lombardi told Hecker on the phone the next day.

That's a pretty good example of how quickly Vince Lombardi went about assembling his coaching staff. Along with Hecker, Phil Bengtson, a seasoned and successful coach with the San Francisco 49ers, was tabbed to coach the defensive squad. For the offense, Lombardi chose John (Red) Cochran to coach the backfield, Tom Fears to direct the receivers, and Bill Austin for the front line. As it was, Lombardi built a staff with both unproven talent and veteran experience. And they were quite an energetic and youthful group at that, averaging thirty-seven years in age. Bengtson, at forty-five, was the oldest, while Austin, only twenty-nine was the youngest.

From the outset, assistant coaches learned that Vince Lombardi did not mince any words. "I demand the best from all of you," he told them. "I'm a perfectionist, and there's absolutely no excuse for anything other than that." And when he sat them all down together to review game films and discuss the players, he'd frequently bark out comments like: "That man can't play in the NFL!" or "Some of our defensive backs are ducking tackles, actually ducking tackles. We want *men* here, not just players. Players are a dime a dozen."

Along those lines, Lombardi made clear the type of people he wanted on his team. He wanted players with desire, he told the coaches, a quality, as he said, that "you can't examine them for . . . [except] under game conditions or perhaps in contact work." He wanted players who ached to get back into action, who "are aggressive even when it hurts . . . who have the pride to make any sacrifice to win."

"Some guys play with their heads," he noted. "That's okay. You've got to be smart to be number one in any business. But more important, you've got to play with your heart, with every fiber of your body. If you're lucky enough to find a guy with a lot of head and a lot of heart, he's never going to come off the field second."

The coaching staff set about first building the Packer defensive squad at Lombardi's direction. "There is nothing more discouraging to a team," he said, "than to watch the opposition run up and down the field at will against you." Regarding individual players, he was looking for men, in particular, who possessed "knowledge, confidence, and self-control." These were required qualities for the defense because, as he said: "Defensive football is a game of abandon, and you have to have the kind of players who will be able to play with abandon, the hell-for-leather types."

By trading players and draft choices, Lombardi built a completely new defensive front four in a relatively brief period of time. He picked up Henry Jordan, Bill Quinlan, and Willie Davis from the Cleveland

Browns and combined them with Packer veteran Dave (Hawg) Hanner to create one of the best front lines in the National Football League. They were light in weight but strong and quick—strong enough to stop the run, quick enough to put pressure on the passer.

Lombardi also put together a formidable defensive backfield that averaged six feet three inches, and 230 pounds. Like the front line, the backfield had strength enough to handle runners and speed enough to cover pass receivers. Emlen Tunnell, a veteran defensive back, was purchased immediately from the New York Giants. With time, Lombardi added such powerful individuals as: Ray Nitschke at middle linebacker, Dan Currie and Bill Forrester at outside linebackers, and Willie Wood, Hank Gremminger, Jesse Whittenton, and Herb Adderly for the secondary.

On offense, Lombardi sought players with intelligence and versatility. "Versatility in an offensive lineman is a plus," he said, "and on my time a must, because you never know when an injury will strip you of one of your linemen." He required "intelligence on the part of all the players" because "the team that cannot execute properly after an audible is called is in deep trouble."

Accordingly, the Packers made early key trades for guard Fred (Fuzzy) Thurston from Baltimore and running back Lew Carpenter from Cleveland. And the Packers gave up a high draft choice to the St. Louis Cardinals for veteran quarterback Lamar McHan. Lombardi liked perennial second-string Packer quarterback Bart Starr—and almost started him. But he opted, instead, to trade for and then start McHan because, psychologically, Starr represented the losing past. A new veteran quarterback, Lombardi reasoned, offered a new beginning with new hope.

In general, though, and strategically, the Packers offense was built around the incredibly versatile and talented Paul Hornung, who did just about everything—including running, passing, receiving, and kicking both field goals and extra points. Lombardi realized that Hornung was not only unusually gifted but also a player who had tremendous drive and courage. He was the kind of player who did what it took to win and therefore, thought Lombardi, would inspire other players on the team to do likewise.

On the other hand, Lombardi cut players who he considered to have losing attitudes. "I don't want any bad apples in my organization," he told a friend. "I get one apple in the bushel over here and the rest of them will start rotting, too."

An early case in point was All-Pro Billy Howton—the second-leading pass receiver in Green Bay's history. Howton had a reputation as being difficult, so Lombardi used him as trade bait, sending him to the Cleveland Browns for Quinlan and Jordan. Similar trades were made or players were cut from the roster "not because they couldn't play football but because they weren't made for my system," explained Lombardi. Others were let go because the coaches felt they would not make the sacrifices necessary to win and "we had to make examples of them."

"I'd rather have a player with fifty percent ability and one hundred percent desire," Lombardi explained, "because the guy with one hundred percent desire you know is going to play every day, so you can make a system to fit into what he can do. The other kind of guy—the guy with one hundred percent ability and fifty percent desire—can screw up your whole system because one day he'll be out there waltzing around."

Once Lombardi felt he had found a player with 100 percent desire, he took care to give that individual a special personal touch. He called Hornung, for example, in the spring of 1959—months before training camp began. "I've been looking at the films, and you're my left halfback," he said. Hornung later recalled that that phone call "was the start of the eight best years of my life . . . Till he [Lombardi] got there, the whole place was so disorganized that, unless I'd been traded, I would've quit football in a year or two."

"Come on out here, Emlen; you can help me out," Emlen Tunnell recalled Lombardi saying to him on the phone. "Nobody else wanted me then. . . . [And] I didn't want to let him down." To Willie Davis, Vince said, "We think you can help us." And veteran Willie Wood termed the first conversation he had with Vince Lombardi as "the most important conversation I ever had with him. He told me that the Packers had initiated the trade, that they felt that I could help . . . , that I was the kind of football player he was looking for."

Both Wood and Davis noted that Lombardi offered them $1,000 more than they were currently making. (They made about $10,000 a year at the time.) Said Wood: "I knew that here was a man who was willing to compensate me before I played one ball game for him. . . . This was a man I wanted to play for."

Once he had his core group of players and coaches assembled, Lombardi set about focusing on teamwork and building team spirit. "You were chosen to be a Green Bay Packer," he told them. And the players took it to heart. "He made it sound like something unique and wonderful," remembered Willie Wood. "We felt that we were a select bunch of people," said Ray Nitschke.

After team dinners, Lombardi had everyone sing songs together. And he instituted one of the first dress codes in professional football where everyone was required to wear dress shirts and ties on trips and at meals—topped off by a green sports coat that had an impressive gold Packer emblem on the breast pocket. "A game day is a business day," he explained—and everyone should dress and act like professionals and champions both "on the field and off."

Teamwork was a prominent word in the vocabulary of Vince Lombardi as a head coach. He wanted the Packers to think of themselves as a unit. He wanted them to possess "selfless teamwork and collective pride," which, as he said, would "accumulate until they have made positive thinking and victory habitual."

"Teamwork is the primary ingredient of success," he'd often say to the players. "People who work together will win, whether it be against complex football defenses or the complex problems of modern society."

Offensive tackle Forrest Gregg recalled that Lombardi "liked the ideas of all the coordination of a vast number of human beings to make a running game work—the interdependence of players." He simply had to have "people mesh and gear smoothly." Moreover, Lombardi put these principles to work in games by running plays that required "all eleven men to play as one to make it succeed." For him, touchdowns were "the result of each man . . . carrying out his assignment perfectly."

When on the practice field, he pounded into them his idea of "teamwork through participation." He liked to "climb up on the back" of "the seven-man blocking sled [as] the offensive line makes the first charge."

"No! No!" he'd holler, before the sled even came to a rest. "Together! Together! Not like a typewriter."

Over the years, Vince focused on keeping his close-knit crew strong. "Our single most important public is our own employees—our team," he said. "For without a skilled, coordinated group of talented people behind us, we haven't a chance in the world of attaining success."

With that principle in mind, he switched players to new positions in an attempt to get the best eleven men into the lineup. He traded aging veterans a year or two before they were over the hill. He brought in new promising draft choices or veterans to shore up key weaknesses. And always, he took time for that "personal touch." In 1965, for instance, when the Packers traded for veteran placekicker Don Chandler, Lombardi sat down with him and went over the whole team, both offense and defense. "He discussed the strengths and weaknesses, the changes he was planning, the problems he'd had in 1964 . . . ," recalled Chandler. "He felt if he'd had a good kicking game, he'd have won the championship."

And in 1969, when Lombardi started all over again with the Washington Redskins, he began virtually the same way he had with the Packers ten years earlier. He hired an offensive backfield coach because of good recommendations. He retained two members of the previous coaching staff because they knew the team personnel and could advise him accordingly. And he brought along a couple of coaches he'd previously worked with, including Bill Austin for the offensive line and Lew Carpenter for the receivers. Lombardi even enticed veteran Sam Huff, who was a player back in Vince's days with the Giants, out of retirement. Huff served as a player-coach and stated to the press that "the only reason I came back to pro football was to be with him."

And Lombardi also traded for or purchased outright six former Packer players. When asked why he had brought to Washington so many of his former coaches and players, Vince was straightforward with his answer. "[The team] must bend or already be molded to your personality," he said. "I've got to have men who *bend* to me."

Vince Lombardi not only found men who would "bend" to him; he found men who would take his advice and play as a team for him. "The year before he got there," recalled Packer receiver Max McGee, "everybody was playing for his own contract and doing what would individually satisfy himself. But after Lombardi came, everybody on the squad worked for the team. I'm convinced of it."

And for all the success he attained, Vince would always credit the way the players worked together. "It's the team!" he'd stress. "Teamwork is what the Green Bay Packers were all about. They didn't do it for the individual glory. They did it because they loved one another."

That's why Lombardi worked so hard year in and year out to pull a strong team together, to choose "100 percent" players with desire and courage, to find those who'd work with one another. That's why at the end of every training camp, after all the final cuts had been made, Vince would turn to his assistant coaches and, with a sigh of relief and a tinge of pride, say: "Gentlemen, we have our team now."

Lombardi Principles

- Build a young, energetic staff with both unproven talent and veteran experience.
- Demand the best from everyone.
- Remember that players are a dime a dozen. Look for individuals with intelligence, versatility, and desire; those who have a lot of heart; those who are aggressive even when it hurts; those who have the pride to make any sacrifice to win.
- Remember that there's nothing more discouraging than to watch the opposition run up and down the field at will against you. Championship teams must stop the run!
- Trade or cut players with losing attitudes.
- When you find that "100 percent desire" individual, take care to give him a special personal touch.
- Try to make the team members feel unique and wonderful—as if they are a special bunch of people.
- Individual commitment to a group effort is what makes a team work, a company work, a civilization work.
- The success of the individual is completely subjected to the satisfaction that he receives in being part of the successful whole.
- Business is a very complex machine, all of whose components are people, and, as in a football team, it is vital that these people mesh and gear smoothly.
- The team must bend or already be molded to your personality. You've got to have people who bend to you.
- People who work together will win.

I would've worked for him for nothing. You couldn't buy an education like I was getting.

NORB HECKER,
ASSISTANT COACH, GREEN BAY PACKERS

He was a genius in his field.
JERRY KRAMER

3   *Know Your Stuff*

Phil Bengtson once commented that Vince Lombardi "had no question about how to do this or how to do that in football." Fuzzy Thurston called Lombardi "a fantastic organizer." Lamar McHan was utterly astonished. "I've never seen a man with such tremendous knowledge of football," he said. "If he'd gone into IBM as a bookkeeper," remarked Don Chandler, "I'm positive he'd be chairman of the board by now." Jerry Kramer simply stated that Lombardi was "a genius in his field."

Having such a great command of his craft provided Vince credibility with players, assistant coaches, fans, and upper management. Because of his extraordinary knowledge and expertise, people respected him and wanted to be around him. Not only did they feel they could learn something, but also, after being with him awhile, they came to believe that he could make them champions.

During his first few years with the Packers, Lombardi overwhelmed people with statistics that often helped prove a point he was trying to make. To justify his rigorous training program and demand that all players be in top physical condition, he stated that "the history of the National Football League has proved that most games are won in the last two minutes of the first half or the second half. And it's usually the team which is best conditioned which usually wins the game."

To encourage 100 percent effort all the time, he lectured: "In a football game, there are approximately one hundred and sixty football plays. And yet there are only three or four players who have anything to do with the outcome of the game. The only problem is that no one knows when those three or four players are coming up. As a result, each and every player must go all out on all one hundred and sixty plays."

In addition to his being a student of the game's history, Lombardi's credibility was enhanced by the fact that he had been an offensive lineman. He'd been battered and beaten in the trenches himself. Therefore, he knew what he was talking about. And Vince played upon his experience for all it was worth. He made it a point to remind his players that he'd been there, done that, experienced what they were currently experiencing. In other words, he had paid the price. "An offensive lineman seldom finds his name in headlines. I know. I was one myself," he told them on many occasions.

Pat Sumerall, placekicker for the Giants under Lombardi, pointed out that Vince "knew every part of the machine—what the ends were supposed to do, what blocks the tackles and guards ought to call. Just a complete command of what he was teaching." Even though he was in charge of the offense when with the Giants, Lombardi made it a point to get to know everything about the defense. Listening to and learning from experts like Tom Landry paid off when Vince got to the Packers, as he frequently held clinics to lecture players and coaches on intricate details of all aspects of football strategy and psychology. One young coach who listened to Vince speak for eight hours on just one play was future Hall-of-Famer John Madden. "That's when I realized I might have a lot to learn about coaching football," said Madden.

"The successful pass rush is designed to do two fundamental things," Lombardi would point out when speaking about defensive strategy, "get to that passer and throw him for a loss—and make that passer lose confidence in his pass protection and demoralize him and with him his team." Moreover, Lombardi would continue, "the successful pass rush is dependent upon: anticipation and quick recognition of the passing situation; quickness and decisiveness in the initial move; and the coordination of the hands, the feet, and the head, with the shoulders forward to prevent the blocker from getting underneath the pass rusher."

If the offensive team elected to institute an end run against the Packers, Lombardi had his men prepared for it. "A team that cannot keep its opponent from running to the outside is a team that has lost the control on which the defense against the running game is founded. So the defense must demolish every end run." But Lombardi would not only *tell* them they must "demolish every end run"; he also *taught them how to do it*. "There are three essentials to good defense against the end run," he'd say calmly. "One: There must be a contain man. Two: There must be a pursuit by the whole defense. Three: There must be a man to check for the option play pass." And thinking of another essential as he went along, he'd add, "Four. There must be angry gang tackling by everybody on that defensive team."

Lombardi coached his players to be attuned to all aspects of the game, including those that did not impact them directly. He wanted his players to understand not just their own positions but their teammates' positions as well. So he would constantly enlighten his defensive players on the intricate differences between specific spots in the lineup, in part, so each could understand the other. "The basic difference between the defensive linemen and linebackers," he'd teach, "is that on the snap of the ball the lineman acts and then diagnoses; the linebacker, on the snap of the ball, diagnoses and then acts. The linebacker never guesses but rather waits for his key. It is far better for him to be a little hesitant than it is to retreat too quickly and do the wrong thing."

And Lombardi would take time to instruct the defense about offensive strategy—and the offense about defensive strategy. For instance, he lectured the members of his offensive team about weaknesses of different pass defenses because, as he said, "it is on a team's ability to exploit those weakness that its success with the passing game will depend." He would discuss the intricate weakness of the man-to-man defense, the weakness of the zone defense, and the weakness of the combination defense. And then he would coach the quarterback to call appropriate plays for the appropriate defenses. Against the zone, he was to throw short passes "underneath the linebackers or over the middle beyond the strong-side linebacker"; against the combination, it was "screens to the halfback" or "flares from the fullback"; and so on, and so on, and so on. For every conceivable defense, Lombardi had a series of plays designed to beat it.

And he also knew, with no uncertainty, what he had to have in a quarterback who would be able to execute all the potential options. "A quarterback must have great poise," said Vince. "He must not be panicked by what the defense does or his own offense fails to do. He must know the characteristic fakes and patterns of his ends and backs and anticipate the break before the receiver makes it. . . . He has to have the quick release [and] the arm to throw the ball."

"If you find all this in one man," said Lombardi, "you have found a special person." On the other hand, he said, "if he can't do that, you just say, 'Son, you'll have to play some other position.'"

Vince Lombardi was also famous for his ability to remember key details about anything and everything related to football or his players. "Coach wanted me to return kickoffs if anything happened to Herb Adderly," recalled running back Chuck Mercein. "I was amused and I asked, 'Why me?' And he said, 'I think you can do it. I've seen you catch them before. . . . You returned them against us.' I was very surprised because I thought nobody ever remembered that I returned kickoffs in the NFL. But he did."

Even Art Rooney, owner of the Pittsburgh Steelers, from a distance saw this ability. "Like a golfer who remembers each shot," he said, "Lombardi remembered all the breaks of the season that went in his favor, fumbles recovered, punts that rolled out-of-bounds instead of into the end zone."

Many people thought that "all these details really had to clutter his thinking," as one player had said. But Lombardi justified his attention to detail. "Football is a game of inches," he argued, "and inches make the champion." So, all through his career, he'd work for hours, even days, on those "inches"—on those small things that would give his team the edge. Back in his days as a high school football coach, for instance, Vince would spend Saturday afternoons during the season meticulously analyzing opposing players. He would go and sit in the stands of St. Cecilia's next opponent and take notes. Then he would present reports to his players on the most minute intricacies of how the other players acted in certain situations. He took the time for it because it invariably gave his players an advantage. "You may not be able to call the exact play but can almost anticipate what they will do," he lectured. "You do this by studying their past history. . . . People don't change what has been working for them."

He could also pick up the most subtle details about people and situations—details that no one else would notice. Such an ability often frustrated him, though. During some games people might hear him screaming on the sidelines. "What the hell's going on out here?" he'd yell to the referees while throwing his notes to the turf. "That's interference! Can't you see it?"

But while his keen eye was often a source of personal frustration, it often helped members of the ball club, who clearly benefited from the subtle nuances in their performances that Vince picked up. For example, when he noticed that receiver Ben Wilson was dropping a few more passes than he ought to, Lombardi sent him to see an eye doctor. "So I did," recalled Wilson, "and the doctor said he was surprised I had *ever* caught a football with those eyes of mine."

Even more interesting was the case of Washington running back Larry Brown. "He noticed [in practice] that I was like one-fiftieth of a second late coming off my stance," related the rookie Redskin.

"What's the matter with you, Brown?" fumed Lombardi. "Are you deaf?!"

When the young running back hung his head and admitted that he was, indeed, partially deaf in his left ear, Lombardi immediately had a doctor check him out and then fitted his helmet with a special hearing aid. And Larry Brown credited the coach for his improved performance, saying that it was Lombardi "who first noticed that I might have a hearing problem."

When the new device was being tested at practice, Vince walked up and bellowed into Brown's ear: "Can you hear me, Larry?"

"Coach, I never had *any* trouble hearing *you!*" quipped the young running back.

Friends and associates also noted that Vince Lombardi's capacity for detail was matched by his intellectual abilities. He not only possessed a penetrating, logical mind that he employed to isolate and solve problems; he also thought deeply about his craft—from the psychological aspects of football to its scientific applications. "Everything in football, as in physics, is relative," said the former high school physics teacher, "and the people you could put on the offense could be every bit as big and just as mobile."

More than that, though, Vince analyzed the sport from a philosophical point of view. Because of football's fierce nature, he argued, it required a kind of discipline "that is seldom found in any other place in this modern world." And he noted that "dancing is a contact sport. Football is a collision sport." It was "violent" and "dangerous," and "to play it other than violently would be imbecilic."

To Lombardi, football was also noble and honorable. "It is a symbol, I think, of what this country's best attributes are," he once said in a speech, "namely, courage, stamina, and coordinated efficiency. It is a Spartan game, and I mean by that, it requires Spartanlike qualities in order to play it, and I am speaking of the Spartan qualities of sacrifice and self-denial rather than that other Spartan quality of leaving the weak to die."

It was obvious to those around him that Vince Lombardi really loved football. He lived it twenty-four hours a day, got emotional about it, thought about its deeper meanings, preached it passionately. And in coaching, in leadership, or in anything else, that kind of passion, knowledge, and dedication just naturally inspire other people.

"He made you a believer," remembered Willie Davis. "He told you what the other team was going to do and he told you what you had to do to beat them, and invariably he was right."

And for a young coach like Norb Hecker, the experience gained by being under Lombardi's wing was invaluable. "I would've worked for him for nothing," said Hecker. "You couldn't buy an education like I was getting."

Lombardi Principles

- Have a great command of your craft to provide credibility with players, assistant coaches, fans, and upper management.
- Be a student of your sport's history. Use statistics to prove your point.
- Remind your players that you, too, were once in the trenches.
- Get to know every part of the machine.
- Do not just *tell* your players to do something; teach them *how* to do it.
- Coach the members of your team to be attuned to all aspects of the game, not just those that impact them directly.
- Enlighten them on the intricate differences between various positions in the lineup so that they will better understand one another.
- Pay attention to details. While, at times, it may frustrate you, it can also pay big dividends for individual players.
- Study your opponent's past history. People don't change what has been working for them.
- Think deeply about your sport—about its psychological, scientific, and philosophical aspects.
- Remember that your own passion, knowledge, and dedication will inspire other people.

To have a good running game, you have to run as a coach. You have to derive more creative satisfaction from the planning and the polishing of the coordination of all eleven men. . . .

VINCE LOMBARDI

Make no little plans. They have no magic to stir men's blood. Make big plans.

VINCE LOMBARDI

4   *Develop a Game Plan*

In 1936, Vince Lombardi was a senior at Fordham University. He was the starting right guard on the football team, which had gone undefeated up until its last game with arch rival New York University. The heavily favored Fordham Rams went into that game expecting to win easily and then advance to play in the Rose Bowl on New Year's Day. But NYU shocked Fordham with a 7–6 upset victory. As a result, there was no Rose Bowl appearance that year, and Vince and thousands of fans and supporters were left with a bitterly disappointing end to a great season.

Twenty-four years later, in Lombardi's second year in Green Bay (1960), the Packers scratched and clawed their way to a Western Conference title. But in the subsequent NFL championship game against the Philadelphia Eagles, the Packers fell short with a 17–13 loss. Again Vince and thousands of other people were left with a bitter disappointment at the end of the season.

The lessons Lombardi took away from those two losses, neither of which he was ever able to get out of his mind, were: 1) never take an easy opponent lightly; and 2) work hard at game preparation.

Because of these hard-learned lessons, game planning and preparation became an ongoing part of his coaching philosophy. More than that, though, Vince was driven to prepare. "When I think of Lombardi," recalled Bill Heinz (a later Packer assistant coach), "I picture him as tense and driving, not only demanding of others, but extraordinarily well prepared."

Lombardi not only had a grand plan for the entire season, but he also made it a point to prepare in meticulous detail for each and every individual game. Take, for instance, the steady ritual he went through to dissect an upcoming opponent: he would study their past games on film, he persuaded others to "scout" them out to gather as much information as possible, he analyzed all aspects of their offenses and defenses, and then he determined their strengths and weaknesses. As a result of all this activity, Lombardi built extensive files on every NFL team he played, kept them updated, and then devised specific plans that he shared with players the week before the scheduled game.

When quarterback Lamar McHan first joined the Packers, he was both astounded and gratified by the intense game preparation. "All of a sudden it was like a road map that was clear," he marveled. "I felt when I went on the field I had some solid ideas to work with."

Paul Hornung described Lombardi's strategy and game preparation as "flawless." "If we were playing the Baltimore Colts," Hornung said, "and we had the ball on the left side of the field between the forty-yard lines, we knew that, on third down, the Colts would throw up a zone defense against us—and we knew exactly how to attack that zone. The quarterback knew which plays to call; the linemen knew how to adjust."

And so it went with every game the Packers played. And since every team was different, every game plan was different. One year, Green Bay confused the Los Angeles Rams by "moving around in the offensive line." Another year, Lombardi surprised the Dallas Cowboys by "having Bart Starr take to the air" on an unusually windy day "when Dallas expected Green Bay to avoid the wind and keep the ball on the ground." And in Super Bowl I, the coach, known for his conservative defenses, shocked the Kansas City Chiefs by having his linebackers charge the quarterback in all-out blitzes that successfully disrupted the offense's flow. That decision was made by Lombardi at halftime after it became apparent that the Chiefs were thwarting his original game plan.

While the Packers devised separate game plans for each opponent, there were also a number of general strategies that were employed on a consistent and regular basis. One general strategy frequently employed, for instance, was to focus on whatever strong points their opponents had. "[His philosophy] was to attack a man at his strength," remembered seven-time All-Pro center Jim Ringo, "and once they were vulnerable the weaker points would come more readily. That's the way we attacked as a *team*." Said Lombardi on this particular strategy: "What you try to do is defeat what they do best. Just like I try to do what I do best and you try to stop it."

A good example of how he successfully made it work was the way his Packers handled the powerhouse Cleveland Browns—whom they never lost to on Lombardi's watch. "[They] had Jim Brown, one of the great runners of all time," remembered Vince, "plus a good passing game and excellent defense. Our defense never let Jim Brown run wild, and one of the reasons was the play of Ray Nitschke. Jim Brown was his responsibility and, in that [1965] championship game, Nitschke made the defensive play to stop Cleveland and seal the championship for us. It was late in the third quarter, we were ahead, but a Cleveland touchdown would give them the lead and the momentum. They were driving and on our forty-yard line when they threw a circle pass to Brown down on the goal line. Nitschke, keying Brown, went all the way with him and batted the ball out of Brown's arms. It was a great play and seemed to take the spirit out of the Browns. We won 23–12. Jim Brown never had a 100-yard day against the Packers."

Vince Lombardi was also a big believer in ball control. "The team that controls the ball controls the game," he would say. But behind those plain words were purposeful actions devoted to the creation of a disciplined running game and an imaginative passing offense. And Lombardi was pretty clear on how he viewed his own role as head coach in that process. "What it comes down to is that to have a good running game, you have to run as a coach," he said. "You have to derive more creative satisfaction from the planning and the polishing of the coordination of all eleven men rather than just three or four."

When Lombardi said, "You have to run as a coach," he meant that coaches must involve themselves with the members of the team; that they have to be an integral part of the preparation, the planning, the polishing of the game plan. And that means working with the players, soliciting their ideas, and participating in the practice sessions. Such a commitment involved a lot of work in the week prior to games when all of the preparation and planning was conceived and completed. But by the time Sunday rolled around, Lombardi usually "did not try to inject strategy from the sideline," according to Paul Hornung. "He felt that should have been done during the week." Rather, Vince let the quarterbacks call their own plays and be the leaders on the field.

All the long hours and hard work around game planning paid off, not only in the team's execution but in the strengthened confidence of each individual player. "[Lombardi] prepared us beautifully for every game, for every eventuality," said Bart Starr. "That—more than words of encouragement—was what built up my self-confidence. Thanks to Coach Lombardi, I knew—I was positive—that I would never face a situation I wasn't equipped to handle."

A critical part of Vince Lombardi's game plan, each and every week, was, quite simply, to win the ball game. To the players, it may have seemed like an obvious, take-it-for-granted part of the plan, but the coach never let them forget that ultimate goal. "I want every man dedicated to the only thing that's important in this league: winning the game," he'd tell them. "At Green Bay, gentlemen, we have winners."

Lombardi also told them that they were going to be a championship team, that *he* expected them to be a championship team, and, moreover, that *they* should expect it of themselves. That was his *long-term* game plan—for them to be champions. And to keep them fired up, he kept saying it to the members of his team—over and over and over again. "Make no little plans," advised Vince Lombardi. "They have no magic to stir men's blood. Make big plans."

Lombardi also believed that "the reach should always exceed the grasp." "I've heard two responses given to the man who is always reaching for the moon," he once said. "The first is that even if he does not reach the moon, he will perhaps catch a star or two, and this is a wonderful thing. The other answer is that the man who keeps reaching for the moon will sooner or later strain himself into a hernia. I tend to believe in catching stars and have been willing to take my chances on the hernia."

Lombardi Principles

- Never take an easy opponent lightly.
- Work hard at game preparation.
- Study your opponents. Gather as much information as possible. Determine strengths and weaknesses.
- Build an extensive file on every opponent and keep these files updated.
- Try to defeat what your opponent does best. Just like I try to do what I do best and my opponents try to stop it.
- Remember that the team that controls the ball controls the game.
- You have to run as a coach.
- Don't try to inject much strategy from the sideline. That should be done during the week. But be prepared to make changes at halftime.
- Use game planning and meticulous preparation to build a player's confidence.
- Make winning a part of your game plan. Articulate that goal each and every week.
- Make no little plans. Make big plans.
- The reach should always exceed the grasp.

One must not hesitate to innovate and change with the times. The leader who stands still is not progressing, and he will not remain a leader for long.

VINCE LOMBARDI

In all my years of coaching, I have never been successful using somebody else's play. . . . It makes you feel that you are losing whatever creativity you have had.

VINCE LOMBARDI

Change is good.

VINCE LOMBARDI

| 5 | ## Encourage Innovation, Imagination, and Creativity |

In the early 1940s, "Mr. Lombardi" stopped several of his football players in the halls of St. Cecilia High School. "I dreamed up a new play," he told them enthusiastically. "I woke up at three in the morning!"

In 1967, his last year as head coach of the Green Bay Packers, "Coach Lombardi put in a new play, a thirty-seven-rollout pass, which no one had ever heard of before," according to Jerry Kramer. "Straight out of the blue, Lombardi just made it up."

From the beginning of his career to the end, Vince Lombardi employed a quality common to all great coaches—imagination. He was an unusually creative and innovative leader who understood that in order to be creative leaders first have to understand all the aspects of their craft—including history, past innovations, details, and nuances. Only then can they break above the fray with something truly different and useful.

In his early days at St. Cecilia, Lombardi strategically set out to learn his craft. He studied football and basketball from books. He spoke with successful coaches, picked their brains, relentlessly asked questions. He also trained to become a referee, passed the required tests, and officiated games. After a while, Lombardi began to do things that were unheard of for high school football coaches in the state of New Jersey.

For example, he implemented the Notre Dame single-wing offense he'd learned in his playing days at Fordham. "It was all we really knew," Vince explained, "and in this coaching business, as in anything else, that's where you have to start." But after a few years, he adopted the T formation—an offense characterized by deception, speed, effective blocking, and a balanced approach. The T had been employed with great success by Clark Shaugnessey at Stanford University and by George Halas with the Chicago Bears. Lombardi was intrigued by it, so he wrote to Shaugnessey and asked him for more detailed information. Lombardi also spoke with other college coaches who were employing it effectively—including his former college coach at Notre Dame, Frank Leahy.

After he figured out all the subtleties of the T formation, he taught it to his players. Surely, reasoned Lombardi, if it worked in college and in the pros, it would work in high school. And he was right, it did work. As a matter of fact, that was a primary reason for the sustained winning streaks of his football teams. In later years, Fr. Timothy Moore of St. Cecilia pointed out that Vince "was the first football coach in our county and maybe in New Jersey to use the T formation."

But that wasn't the only innovation implemented at St. Cecilia. In 1943, Lombardi created a preseason training camp for his football play-ers. Even though this was something that just wasn't done by other high schools, Lombardi insisted his players attend. To cover costs, he had them raise ten dollars each by selling candy door-to-door. And once it began, "Vince ran the camp like the army," recalled Father Moore. The players got up early in the morning, had breakfast together, went to mass, put in two hours of calisthenics and practice, had lunch, partici-pated in a three-hour afternoon practice session, had supper, and then turned in by 10:00 P.M.

During his nine years at St. Cecilia, Lombardi was always trying something new, always experimenting with new ideas that might give his team a winning edge. "Tim, I've got a new system!" he'd announce to Father Moore. And then, "we'd have a new offense the next week."

People around Vince Lombardi often commented that he "had a bril-liant mind," that it "was always going," that he was fascinated with new technology, and that he "had a lot of little kid in him." A new idea could hit him anywhere, so he often scribbled notes on the back of envelopes or other scraps of paper he might find lying around. At restaurants, he would diagram plays on napkins or tablecloths. During games, he'd "prowl the sidelines like a caged tiger"—always keeping his eyes focused on the players, watching carefully, looking for something he could augment, expand, or enhance.

"From our first conversation," remembered West Point coach Red Blaik, "I could tell that he had a good knowledge of the game, that he had much more than just an ordinary mentality, that he had an unusual amount of imagination." Blaik couldn't know then, but by the time Lombardi left West Point he would have helped Army become the first college football team to employ closed-circuit television on the sidelines during a game. "That was a long time ago and nobody ever did that," Vince recalled in later years. "[But] they outlawed it! They thought I was getting an advantage. Anybody else could get the same advantage, but nobody else understood what the hell they were doing, so they said, 'The hell with it. Nobody can use it.'"

And the innovations continued when Lombardi signed up with the New York Giants. For instance, Lombardi placed a scout up in the press box, armed him with a Polaroid camera, instructed him to take pictures during the game, and then had him lower the pictures down to the field in an old sock attached to a string. Fans wondered what in the world was going on. But Lombardi justified his unusual tactic by touting the value of pictures over words. "Visual education is much better than telling the quarterback the defenses," he said.

When he arrived at Green Bay, Lombardi kept experimenting with film and video analysis. He videotaped practice sessions and added wide-angle projections to the cameras, which allowed his coaches to view the entire playing area. "It was a tremendous advantage over the old way," he explained, because the "cameraman was often fooled by the play and you couldn't get the whole picture."

Lombardi also built new offices in Green Bay and computerized the entire Packer organization. He installed a new electric grid piping system under the turf at Lambeau Field to prevent the ground from freezing. He dreamed up new offensive alignments that changed the game for players at certain positions. He figured out new ways to beat zone and man-to-man coverage. And he also instituted several new types of blocking methods. "Do-Dad" blocking, for example, enabled "three men (two guards and center on offense) to handle four defensive players," as Vince explained it. And "Rule" blocking, he said, "allowed the offensive line to adjust to all defenses [and] simplified line play."

As general manager, Lombardi also ran the future of the team creatively. After several years, for instance, he had successfully accumulated a number of high draft picks, which, in turn, he used to pick college players in their junior year—despite the fact that they had their senior year to go. This tactic was dubbed redshirting. Because of it, in essence, the Packers were getting the jump on other teams in the draft. But when some franchises began to complain that this was an unfair advantage, the National Football League banned the drafting of redshirts until the players had completed their college eligibility.

Vince Lombardi's most famous innovation at Green Bay was, undoubtedly, the offensive play that came to be known as the "Lombardi Power Sweep." "[It] was from his own imagination," commented Assistant Coach Phil Bengtson. "Nobody else had used that play and everybody does now." Actually, though, Lombardi first saw it employed as a Fordham player when Coach Jock Sutherland's teams at the University of Pittsburgh ran it. Even though Vince did not invent the play, his innovative style made it better, even perfected it—twenty-five years after he had first seen it.

The Sweep was a powerful offensive weapon where all eleven men moved out in one direction in a well-choreographed "pull and flow." Bart Starr explained that Lombardi diagrammed all its intricacies on the chalkboard while "raising his elbows, gritting his teeth, just bursting with enthusiasm."

"What we try to do is create an alley," explained the coach. "It really has two holes. That's one of the great advantages of this play." Then he'd proceed to explain how the guards pulled out in the direction of play, how the quarterback pivots and hands off to the halfback, how the flanker blocks the defensive safety; that it's the responsibility of the tight end to handle the outside linebacker, and the onside back to block the defensive end, and so on, until all the positions had their assignments. Lombardi regarded it as his best play because, as he said, "all eleven men play as one to make it succeed and that's what *team* means."

In practice, "he would work on that Sweep until the players just could not run it anymore," remembered one assistant coach. And, once implemented, it became so effective that, after a while, the other NFL teams could recognize when it was called but would be unable to stop it. "There's nothing spectacular about it," explained Lombardi. "It's just a ground gainer. . . . You hear those linebackers and defensive backs yell, 'Sweep!' and you can see their eyes almost pop out when they see those guards turning upfield and coming after them."

Lombardi, the coach, valued his Power Sweep for much more than simply the great yard gainer it was. "Continued success with the play, of course, makes for a number one play," he explained, "because from that success stems your confidence, and behind that is the basic truth that it expresses the coach as a coach and the players as a team and they feel complete satisfaction when they execute it and it's completely right."

In general, Vince Lombardi simply liked the idea of trying something new. "Change is good," he once said. But he was wary of short-term change that was not well planned or well thought through. "In football, as in anything else, if you alter your personality just to accomplish something, you're not being true. You're being dishonest. . . . I've seen coaches who, seeing that someone had success with something, immediately tried to take it for themselves. It didn't work because it didn't fit them. It didn't express their personalities. . . . Surprise [rather] should be based on deception and rapidity of maneuver and not radical change."

Lombardi's philosophy surrounding long-term change was quite the opposite, however. "Everything I learned in the 1930s has gone out the window," he stated in later years. And, over the years, he learned that if he didn't strive to innovate, then "someone else *will* come up with that better thing.

"One must not hesitate to innovate and change with the times," he said. "The leader who stands still is not progressing, and he will not remain a leader for long."

The truth is that Vince Lombardi not only *adjusted* to promising modern trends; he actually *created* those new trends in many instances. And he did so not only with his own imagination but also with the help of all the members of his team. During game film skull sessions, for example, there were tremendous free-flowing discussions. One observer noted that Lombardi encouraged "a great interplay of ideas and philosophies with his players" and that, in response, the players would "suggest things that could be done and things that couldn't be done."

When other NFL coaches saw that the Green Bay Packers' innovations worked and that the team was winning, they employed them in their own franchises. "I get a kick out of watching the other teams today because we put a lot of stuff into this league," Vince once remarked. "The Sweep, Do-Dad blocking, the passing game, the idea of reading the defense—a lot of teams are using our passing game. And some of them have beaten us with it."

For an innovative coach like Vince Lombardi, that was part of the price he had to pay for success. He knew that others would steal his ideas, make them their own, try to refine and perfect them. But in a way, it was also a kind of honor. "Imitation is the sincerest form of flattery," as the adage goes.

The only way for creative coaches to succeed, then, is to keep right on being innovative and imaginative. Ultimately, they have to come up with new ideas that outdo and beat their previous innovations.

And so it goes. Just as Vince Lombardi did, any leader must create and innovate every day, all the time, until retirement. "In all my years of coaching," Lombardi said in reflection, "I have never been successful using somebody else's play. . . . [To imitate] makes you feel that you are losing whatever creativity you have had."

Lombardi Principles

- Dream up new plays.
- In order to be creative, first understand all the aspects of your craft—its history, its past innovations, its details and nuances.
- Once you create a new system, implement it right away.
- Have a lot of little kid in you.
- Write down a new idea wherever and whenever it occurs to you.
- Visual education is much better than simply talking to people.
- From success stems confidence.
- Change is good.
- If you alter your personality just to accomplish something, you're not being true. You're being dishonest.
- Surprise should be based on deception and rapidity of maneuver, not radical change.
- If you don't strive to innovate, someone else will come up with that better thing.
- If you stand still, you are not progressing and will not remain a leader for long.
- Involve the members of your team in the creative process.
- Part of the price you must pay for success is watching others steal your ideas.
- Ultimately, come up with new ideas that outdo your previous innovations.

In 1960, the Green Bay Packers finished the regular season with an 8–4 record and won the Western Conference title. But Vince Lombardi, in only his second year with the Packers, was not satisfied with the effort and expressed concern over his team's performance. "We should have won more games," he lamented, "but the people on this team just aren't accustomed to winning. They don't think like winners; they think they were lucky. That'll change. We have the makings here. I need some replacements, and I need to convince the rest of them that they are supposed to win."

The NFL championship game was played the day after Christmas in Philadelphia against the Eagles, who had won the Eastern Conference with a 10–2 record. Despite being on the road and having a worse record, Green Bay was favored to win.

The Packers jumped out to a 6–0 lead with two first-quarter field goals. But veteran Eagle quarterback Norm Van Brocklin threw a touchdown pass to receiver Tommy McDonald and then followed up with a drive that culminated in a field goal. As a result, Philadelphia took a 10–6 lead into the locker room at halftime.

In the third quarter, Green Bay quarterback Bart Starr put the Packers back on top, 13–10, when he capped a sustained drive with a touchdown pass to receiver Max McGee. But in the fourth quarter, Philadelphia mounted a drive of their own to score a touchdown and regain the lead, 17–13.

With less than two minutes remaining on the clock, the Packer offense got the ball on their own thirty-five-yard line and began a determined drive toward the Philadelphia end zone. They made it all the way to the Eagles' nine-yard line, where, as time expired, running back Jim Taylor was tackled by Philadelphia defender Chuck Bednarik. The game ended then and there—and the Green Bay Packers had lost their first NFL championship game under Coach Vince Lombardi. Final score: 17–13.

In the Green Bay locker room after the game, the Packer players were dejected. Some were even crying. When Lombardi addressed them, he did so in a soothing voice and without criticism. "Perhaps you didn't realize that you could have won this game," he said calmly. "We are men and we will never let this happen again. Now we can start preparing for next year."

And Bob Skoronski, who was sitting in the locker room that day, remembered years later that Lombardi was true to his word. "We never lost another play-off game," he said.

PART II
Building Trust

You've got to win the hearts of the people you lead.
VINCE LOMBARDI

You have to sell yourself to the group. And in order to sell yourself to the group, there is no way you can be dishonest about it. Therefore, what you sell has to come from the heart, and it has to be something you really believe in.

VINCE LOMBARDI

I hold it more important to have the players' confidence than their affection.

VINCE LOMBARDI

He asked us to believe in him.

BART STARR,
QUARTERBACK, GREEN BAY PACKERS

6   *Sell Yourself*

All-Pro offensive lineman Forrest Gregg once told a story about Vince Lombardi's first full practice with the Green Bay Packers in 1959. "Vince was over with the quarterbacks, the backs, and the receivers," recalled Gregg. "One of the receivers went out for a pass. He was a heck of a football player but had a tendency to loaf in practice. . . . He was about twenty yards down the field, and he evidently didn't run the pass pattern as precisely as Coach Lombardi wanted, because the coach started yelling at him and he kept yelling until the player had returned to the huddle. The year before, nothing had ever been said to that player by any coach, no matter how much he loafed or goofed off. That sold me on Lombardi."

As this incident demonstrates, Vince Lombardi wasn't afraid to confront a player when he felt that an issue needed to be addressed. And he often yelled, screamed, ranted, and raved when he did so. But interestingly enough, Lombardi coupled such gruff treatment with a strategic effort to sell himself to each and every individual member of the team.

In essence, he made every effort to build trust with his players so that his confrontational yelling would be taken in stride.

"The first thing you have to do is sell yourself," he once advised a group of high school coaches. "That's the number-one objective you must have. In order to sell yourself to the group, there is no way you can be dishonest about it. Therefore, what you sell has to come from the heart, and it has to be something that you really believe in. That belief can be anything. It can be just the plain belief in the game of football. That belief can be in the United States of America as a great democracy. That belief can be in the school itself that you represent."

Vince Lombardi's endeavor to sell himself to the Green Bay Packers' players began well before formal practices began. For instance, he sent out several early squad letters to every member of the team and took special care to make certain the first one was worded very carefully. "I must have rewritten it ten or twelve times," he recalled, "trying to tell what I hoped to do and how I hoped to do it without making it sound like I was setting up a slave-labor camp."

"He asked us to believe in him," remembered Bart Starr of Lombardi's first speech to the group. "He asked all of us to believe in his system. To believe that if we did things the way he wanted them done . . . we would have a winning football team. He said he wasn't sure how long it would take us, but he could guarantee we would win."

As a coach, Lombardi strategically focused on winning the confidence of each and every man on his team. And he was quite clear about what he was seeking from them—and what he wasn't seeking. "I hold it more important to have the players' confidence than their affection," he explained to a friend.

In general, Lombardi sold himself to the players in six key ways:

1. | HE WAS HONEST AND SINCERE:

"I trust you," Vince told Paul Hornung before the first Packer season began. "I just don't want you to let me down."

By trusting his players and by openly telling them that he did, in fact, trust them, Lombardi was building, hoping for, and seeking *their* trust. More important, however, was the simple fact that Vince Lombardi was honest with the members of his team—whether he was dealing with them on a professional or personal basis.

"I never tell a football team anything that I don't absolutely believe myself," he said. "I always tell them the truth. I can't even try to deceive them, because they'd know. I'd know, so they'd know."

2. | HE WAS ENTHUSIASTIC AND PASSIONATE:

Bart Starr described Lombardi as "dynamic," "vibrant," and "full of enthusiasm." Frank Gifford noted that "his enthusiasm, his spirit, was infectious." And Earl Blaik credited Lombardi's "magnetism" as one reason for his success. "[Vince] may have learned a few things during our years together," said Blaik. "But he didn't learn that magnetism at West Point. It was always in him. You don't put magnetism into people."

Moreover, when Vince Lombardi constantly conveyed a passionate belief in himself and his system—or when he simply smiled and said: "This is going to be a winning team"—he was on the road to inspiring those around him. A former teacher at St. Cecilia High School once pointed out that when Lombardi was a teacher there "the kids liked him—and that's motivation in any classroom."

And Lombardi himself said as much. "To win the hearts of the people you lead," he said, "the personality of the individual . . . the incandescence . . . has to do it."

3. | HE GAVE CREDIT WHERE CREDIT WAS DUE AND TOOK RESPONSIBILITY FOR FAILURES:

Repeatedly and throughout his career, Vince Lombardi took responsibility when his team lost games—especially in front of the public and the press. After the 1960 championship game loss to Philadelphia, Lombardi went before reporters and said: "I thought I had them ready. I'll just have to work harder."

On Thanksgiving Day of 1962, the Green Bay Packers were smashed and humiliated in a devastating loss to the Detroit Lions. It was to be the Packers' only loss in a season that culminated with the NFL championship. After the game, Lombardi stated matter-of-factly, "I take all the blame for that one. It was coaching stupidity."

By contrast, after every major victory, Vince inevitably would give credit to everyone else he could think of. After Super Bowl II, for instance, an emotional Lombardi repeatedly thanked the

Packer players, coaches, staff, and his family. "I do not stand alone," he told a national television audience.

And Coach Lombardi regularly took time to speak to his players to make certain they realized how much he knew what they were doing was helping the team. A good example was the manner in which he dealt with players who played on the offensive line—the position he had played at Fordham University. He knew these men frequently played without praise from the press, so he made it a point to stress "that without them there is no glory for the backs and the receivers." Therefore, he stated, "it is imperative that the coach give those linemen all the credit they deserve. The newspapers and television broadcasters never will. I know."

4. | HE STOOD UP FOR THE MEMBERS OF HIS TEAM:

When a writer for the *Saturday Evening Post* took a cheap shot at Green Bay running back Jim Taylor by writing that he was "unsophisticated," "talks in clichés," and "thinks in circles," Lombardi jumped to his player's defense. He publicly pointed out that Taylor quickly grasped instructions and never missed his assignments. "Jim Taylor is one of the most intelligent backs I have ever coached," he said flatly.

Nor was Vince Lombardi afraid to defend people if he felt they were being unfairly demeaned or ridiculed. As a matter of fact, it was part of his leadership philosophy to speak out even if it meant placing his reputation in jeopardy. "Good God, man! Don't you realize that these men are artists?" he once screamed at a labor meeting speaker who degraded football players. "You're not dealing with a bunch of hod carriers or truck drivers. These men are artists, skilled artists, dammit!"

"The leader must be honest with himself." Vince Lombardi once wrote, "and must identify with and back up the group even at the risk of displeasing his superiors."

5. | HE MAINTAINED INFORMAL CONTACT WITH HIS TEAM:

Lombardi frequently stressed that a coach's contact with his team must be "close," "informal," and "sensitive." And that's a piece of advice he practiced as well as preached.

Key Green Bay Packer players were invited over to the Lombardi home every Thursday night during the regular season to have a spaghetti dinner and a relaxed conversation about the upcoming game. Members of his staff found that Vince would often "stop by my desk and we'd just sit there and chat." And during training camp he'd visit the players in their rooms and ask their opinions about his strategy or simply make small talk.

"He'd give everybody hell all day long," remembered veteran Emlen Tunnell, "and then he'd come around to the rooms at night and chew the fat for five or ten minutes. Every night, he'd pick out a different room—a rookie's, a veteran's, made no difference—and he'd stop in and play a hand of cards or two, or just pat a couple of guys on the head, or say something nice, and then he'd leave. And everybody'd say, 'Damn, that man can't be that bad.'"

6. | HE SET A GOOD EXAMPLE:

Prior to Lombardi taking over, previous Packer head coaches would order all players to arrive for breakfast at 7:30 A.M. during training camp. But they themselves would usually not get up early enough to be there. As a result, members of the team frequently did not show up. But when Vince Lombardi instituted precisely the same rule, he made it a point to never miss a breakfast. As a result, the players always had perfect attendance.

Moreover, men who played for Lombardi have consistently commented that he was always out in the field, that "he took the dirty jobs himself," that "he demanded at least as much of himself as he did anyone else," and that "he didn't force us to do anything he wouldn't do himself." Tony Canadeo, a member of the Packer executive committee, stated that Vince "was the type of general who couldn't fight a war from his desk. He had to be down on the field with us, with his people, yelling."

When with the New York Giants, Frank Gifford observed that Lombardi would "eat dinner with us on the road and laugh with us when we won and die with us when we lost." And Green Bay Packer defensive lineman Henry Jordan recalled the time that Vince purchased a new weight machine. "He told us he wanted us to go in there and lift two hundred and fifty pounds every day," recalled Jordan. "He was in there every day, too. Maybe he'd only lift twenty-five pounds, but he'd be in there. He showed us he believed in it, for himself as well as for us."

More telling, however, was a comment from Vince's wife, Marie Lombardi. "He never missed a practice," she said. "Never!"

| | |

Many men who played for Lombardi pointed out that he was "a cut above" other coaches because he was "a supersalesman," because he obtained production from his players "by selling himself to us and us to ourselves," and because he had "a knack for selling his system and his ideas to football players." "Each day he sells the team," said Washington Redskin defensive back Pat Fischer. "He's leading up to the right moment to clinch the sale, and that's supposed to be on Sunday. That's the day we buy."

It was, in part, Lombardi's ability to combine tough discipline with a trustworthy disposition that caused members of his team to follow him. "Men respond to leadership in a most remarkable way," Vince once remarked.

Forrest Gregg was a perfect example of how correct Lombardi was. "This was the kind of coach I wanted," said Gregg. "I want somebody who, when a ballplayer loafs, is going to chew him out; when he doesn't perform as he's capable of, he's going to get chewed out; and if he puts out the effort and tries as hard as he can, he'll be appreciated."

Lombardi Principles

- Make every effort to build trust with your players so that your yelling will be taken in stride.
- Ask the members of your team to believe in you.
- It's more important to have the players' confidence than their affection.
- Never tell your team anything that you don't believe yourself.
- Always tell your team the truth. Don't even try to deceive them. They'll know.
- Take all the blame for a big loss. After you win a big one, be sure to let everybody know that you do not stand alone.
- Give those linemen all the credit they deserve.
- Be honest with yourself.
- Identify with and back up the group even at the risk of displeasing your superiors.
- A coach's contact with his team must be close, informal, and sensitive.
- Demand at least as much of yourself as you do of anyone else.
- Laugh with the team when they win, and die with them when they lose.
- Never miss a practice. Never.
- Combine tough discipline with a trustworthy disposition.

Some need a whip and others a pat on the back and others are better off
when they are ignored.

VINCE LOMBARDI

He was able to bring out the most in people.

TOM LANDRY,
ON VINCE LOMBARDI

Battles are won primarily in the hearts of men.

VINCE LOMBARDI

7   *Treat People As Individuals*

"Hi, I'm Vince Lombardi, and you're my halfback."

Those were Lombardi's first words to New York Giant running back Frank Gifford in 1954. Gifford, who had endured a difficult season the previous year and was contemplating an early retirement, recalled being extraordinarily impressed. "They were the most important words anybody ever said to me in football," he stated. "I had never been anyone's halfback." Gifford kept playing for the Giants and eventually blossomed under Lombardi's leadership of the Giant offense.

Five years later, in 1959, on his first day in training camp as head coach of the Packers, Lombardi said virtually the same thing to Paul Hornung: "You're my running back. The only way you can get out of the job is to get killed." Hornung, like Gifford, appreciated the remark and flourished. In fact, Hornung went on to become an NFL legend.

In contrast to the positive encouragement offered Gifford and Horning, Ray Nitschke was constantly hammered by Lombardi. As a matter of fact, the verbal abuse was so bad that one player described the six-three, 235-pound Packer linebacker as "Vince's whipping dog." And yet Nitschke, too, prospered, to a point where eventually he became one of the greatest middle linebackers in the history of the National Football League.

Lombardi brought out the best in people, in part because he took time to get to know the members of his team as individuals—especially the intricacies of what made them tick, what made them go the limit or stop dead in their tracks, what inspired them or depressed them. "A ball club is made up of as many different individuals as there are positions on it," said Lombardi. And because of this simple fact, it was obvious to him that there were "limitations imposed by the differences in physical ability and mentality."

When it came to details regarding his players, Vince Lombardi was always interested. He kept his ear to the ground, paid attention to every rumor, and watched for subtle nuances in body language or facial expressions. He talked to every person individually, sized him up, figured out each player's inner workings, and then determined how best to work with them.

He observed little things that other, average coaches might not notice or even care about. He knew, for instance, that Bob Skoronski had a "great interest in the stock market," that Boyd Dowler didn't "swear, smoke, drink, or gamble," that Max McGee had a great "ability to relax" because he was "not a perfectionist," and that Bart Starr was "tense by nature" because he *was* "a perfectionist."

In 1962, when author W. C. Heinz was having trouble getting Lombardi on track to fashion the book they were writing together, he instinctively asked Vince to focus on the members of his team. "Okay, I'm going to start naming players," said Heinz. "When I give you a name, you tell me the first thing that comes to your mind about them, not as a player, but as a person."

Heinz ran off the names of all thirty-six Packers. In part, here are a few of Lombardi's comments:

On Forrest Gregg: "Intelligent. Gives you a one-hundred-percent effort, a team player. Quick temper. I've seen him go at teammates in practices. Has all the emotions, from laughter to tears. Can take criticism anywhere, if it's constructive."

On Jim Taylor: "Uses jive talk that I can't understand. Has a lot of desire . . . wants to be the best. He likes to knock people down and he'll go out of his way to do it. You have to keep after him, though."

On Henry Jordan: "All-Pro, all-everything, but don't ever flatter him. He needs public criticism. Needs to be upset to perform. In reviewing [film], I'll make him a target, not to impress somebody else, as you do with some of them, but to help him."

On Willie Davis: "A hell of a young man. Very excitable under game conditions. Before a game he's got that worried look, so I try to bolster his confidence."

On Jerry Kramer: "Nothing upsets him, so you can bawl him out anytime. He's been near death, but he's happy-go-lucky, like a big kid. Takes a loss quite badly, though."

On Paul Hornung: "Can take criticism in public or anywhere. You have to whip him a little. He had a hell-with-you attitude, a defensive perimeter he built around himself when he didn't start out well here. As soon as he had success, he changed. Always looks you straight in the eye."

On Bart Starr: "Modest. Tends to be self-effacing, which is usually a sign of lack of ego. He calls me 'sir.' Seems shy, but he's not. He's just a gentleman. You don't criticize him in front of others. When I came here he lacked confidence and support."

Bart Starr is one Packer who, by his own acknowledgment, probably never would have been inducted into the NFL Hall of Fame if not for Vince Lombardi. Starr was a seventeenth-round draft pick out of the University of Alabama and, by the time Lombardi arrived in Green Bay, was only a bench-warming third-string quarterback. But Vince liked the young man's work ethic and natural abilities. "You can't teach anticipation and instinct," he noted of Starr. So Vince set out to establish a trusting relationship with Bart—and build up his self-confidence, which, Lombardi believed, was Starr's fundamental problem.

"I got to know him, really, in the small meetings we'd have every

Wednesday, Thursday, and Friday morning," recalled Starr. "It was kind of casual, more like a father-and-son discussion . . . than a lecturer and a listener."

Inspired by his coach, Starr put in long hours at practice and worked diligently to improve. His progress was slow going, however, and Lombardi chose to start Lamar McHan at quarterback at the beginning of the season. But by the ninth game, with the team struggling and McHan both inconsistent and sometimes injured, Lombardi gave Starr the lead job. The Packers immediately started winning.

"I made a mistake," Lombardi finally said to Starr. "I want to tell you right now, though, that there aren't going to be any more changes. You are going to be my quarterback." After the season was over, the Packers traded Lamar McHan away. And Bart Starr went on to lead his teams to five world championships and become one of the most successful quarterbacks in NFL history.

Lombardi viewed football's quarterback position as an extension of himself. After all, quarterbacks are the leaders on the field when the action is taking place. All a coach can do during a game is direct from the sidelines. So he strategically sought to build a close relationship with his starting quarterbacks. And he not only did so with Bart Starr in 1959; he also made it a point to create a strong bond with Sonny Jurgensen in 1969 upon taking over the helm of the Washington Redskins.

Lombardi met privately with Jurgensen in the off-season—in February, well before training camp and well before he spoke with any of the other players. "I've heard a lot of things about you as a person and as a player, and I'm sure you've heard a lot of things about me," he told Sonny. "Well, that's got nothing to do with our relationship. I just ask one thing of you: I want you to be yourself. Don't emulate anyone else. Don't try to be someone you're not. Just be yourself."

Lombardi was really trying to let his new quarterback know that he did not expect him to try to be just like Bart Starr. And Jurgensen surely got the message. But after those reassuring words, Vince delivered a fairly stern warning. "I'm going to be tougher on you than anyone else on this football team," he said, "because you're the leader."

Jurgensen later recalled that he "felt like running into a wall, anything to let [Lombardi] know that I would do whatever he wanted of me." Prior to 1969, Sonny Jurgensen had endured seven straight losing seasons. But that year, under Vince Lombardi, Sonny not only led the Redskins to a winning season; he also completed 62 percent of his passes and was the league leader in passing.

But while Lombardi could forge close relationships with some players, he could also maintain distance from others. Personalities dictated not only the extent of relationships but also the manner in which Lombardi sought to motivate people. "Some need a whip and others a pat on the back," he said, "and others are better off when they are ignored."

"[Vinnie] geared himself according to the man," remembered Gifford. "If he felt a specific ballplayer needed to be chewed out, well then, that poor ballplayer was going to be chewed out continuously until he came across. I've seen him ride players; I've seen him ignore players; I've seen him pat them on the fanny. I really can't recall his ever making a bad error in judgment as to how to get the most out of the ballplayer to win the football game. And for Vinnie, that's what it was all about."

Learning about the intricacies of the people on his team was, for Lombardi, an ongoing process—as important to him as the subtle details of the game of football. Yet as he said, it could be "maddening" to try to figure everyone out. "There are many people here it took me a [long] time to find out how far I could push," he once said.

And "push" he did. It was not uncommon around Green Bay Packer practices to hear Vince Lombardi screaming at his players. "We don't need you!" he'd bark at Mike Manuche. "I can go down to the high school and find guys who wouldn't drop balls!" he'd yell at Boyd Dowler. "You're running in mud!" he would shout to Don Chandler. "If you can't do better than that, we'll get somebody else!"

A few individuals would outwardly react to such negative comments. "Go ahead and get somebody else!" Chandler screamed back.

"Get off my back or get yourself another fullback!" an angry Mel Triplett yelled after Lombardi berated him during a review of game films.

"I won't get off your back!" Vince bellowed in retort. "You get paid to play this game." As the roomful of players fell silent, Lombardi whispered to an assistant coach, "I intended to make [Mel] mad, but I didn't mean to make him *that* mad."

Wide receiver Max McGee noted that Lombardi found out quickly that "I didn't play so well if I was being screamed and hollered at. If he'd been on me all the time, like he was [on some others], I'd have quit. I'd have gone someplace else."

Bob Brunet, a veteran Washington Redskin running back, actually walked off the practice field and refused to return. Brunet resented Lombardi's methods and told reporters as much. "Things that are said stay with me all day and all night," he said. "I've had it."

Usually, though, Vince did not allow things to progress to that point. His goal was to motivate his players—not run them off. So when he realized that harsh methods didn't work with a player, he'd quickly change his approach—as he did, for instance, with left linebacker Dan Currie.

"Where criticism just bounces off Ray Nitschke it cuts so deep into Currie that I have to be careful," noted Lombardi. "My first year here I chewed him out in front of the others just once and I knew immediately that he resented it and that it wouldn't help. Even in private you have to be careful how you handle him, but if you tell him he's playing well he'll go out there and kill himself for you."

When Lombardi did make a mistake, he would usually send a message that he was sorry by, as some of the players said, "nudging me a little," or "telling a horrible joke," or "jauntily putting his arm around me and saying something nice." After an argument with Redskin running back Larry Brown, for instance, Vince eased the tension by saying, "You can get mad at me, Larry. You can call me anything you want to call me, but don't say it when I'm around because then you're challenging me, and I'm the head coach."

Max McGee recalled proudly that once he had Lombardi's respect, he never had to participate in the Packers' grueling nutcracker drill. "I didn't even like thinking about that drill," said McGee. "So when he put it in I went up to him and said, 'Coach, I'm not a hitter. I can sweep-block for you, but it will not do me any good to get in the nutcracker drill and get up against Ray Nitschke and have Nitschke hit me with a forearm. You're not gaining anything by having me do that.'"

Lombardi responded to McGee by saying that he couldn't show any partiality. "So you just get in line for that drill, and when you get near the front of the line, turn around and sneak to the end."

"I did that for nine years," remembered McGee. "I never once did the nutcracker drill. We had that agreement."

Because of similar gestures, tailored specifically for a team member's individual needs, Packer players tended to give everything they had for their coach. "He can get that extra ten percent out of an individual," said McGee of Lombardi. "Multiply ten percent times forty men on a team times fourteen games a season—and you're going to win."

And Vince himself explained that focusing on each individual person was, indeed, part of his coaching strategy. "One player can win a football game," he said. "One game can make a season and one player, any player, can make the difference between winning and losing."

And yet Lombardi knew that he, as a leader, could only do so much. The players had to take responsibility for their own performances. They had to have a certain amount of self-motivation. They had to be the ones who were committed to winning and working as a team. "The amount that can be consumed and executed by a team is controlled by the weakest man on it," he said, "and while others can give him physical help, he has to do his own thinking." Of Ray Nitschke, whom Lombardi perennially scolded as a father would scold a son, he said, "You don't improve him, but, happily, he improves himself."

Vince Lombardi's core philosophy for working with individuals can really be summed up in three sentences: "Battles are won primarily in the hearts of men," he said. "Once you win a team's heart, they'll follow you anywhere; they'll do anything for you. . . . You've got to win the hearts of the people you lead."

Lombardi Principles

- A team is made up of as many different individuals as there are positions on it.
- When it comes to details regarding your players, keep your ear to the ground. Remember little things that other leaders might not notice.
- There are patterns of behavior that we can recognize in our employees that may help us, but each individual or group of individuals has facets that must be treated on an individual or group basis, with the usual stereotype rules thrown out the window.
- Build strong bonds with the key team leaders.
- Admit it when you make a mistake.
- Inspire and motivate according to the personality of the individual.
- Learning about the intricacies of the people on your team is as important as the subtle details of your profession.
- Remember that most people want to be independent and dependent all at the same time, to assert themselves and at the same time be told what to do.
- The amount that can be consumed and executed by a team is controlled by the weakest link on it.
- Each individual player has to do his own thinking and take responsibility for his own performance. A leader does not improve an individual; the individual improves himself.
- Battles are primarily won in the hearts of men.

If you're black or white, you're part of the family. We make no issue over a man's color. I just won't tolerate anybody in this organization making it an issue. We respect every man's dignity, black or white.
VINCE LOMBARDI

Any kind of separatism is bad, in football or anywhere else. . . .
VINCE LOMBARDI

8   *Be Color-blind*

In the early 1960s, a New York sportswriter asked Vince Lombardi how many black players were on the Green Bay Packers.

"I can tell you how many players I have on the squad and I can tell you which ones aren't going to be here next year," he responded. "But I can't tell you how many are black and how many are white."

"Come on!" responded the reporter in disbelief.

"I'm not saying I don't know who's black and who's white on the club," continued Lombardi. "I'm just saying that I have no sense of it when I'm dealing with my people."

It was an unusual comment coming from a head coach in professional football during the heart of the American civil rights movement. Most coaches would have just given the reporter the number of black players on their squads and let it go at that, hoping to avoid any controversy.

During that era, the National Football League experienced some serious problems with racial equality. The vast majority (more than 75 percent) of NFL football players were white. There was discrimination in salary and playing positions. There was separation of whites and blacks at meals and hotels. In many NFL franchise cities, black athletes had difficulty finding housing comparable to that of their white team-mates. And many white ballplayers and coaches were bigoted. As a matter of fact, the St. Louis Cardinals were almost ripped apart by a group of white supremacists on the team.

But there were no such troubles on the Green Bay Packers because Vince Lombardi would not permit it.

Several Packer players reported that, in the very first team meeting on the playing field (in 1959), Lombardi called everybody together to make his point. "Listen up," he said. "If I ever hear any man on this squad use the words *nigger* or *dago* or *kike* or any other derogatory racial slur, you're through with this team. If you're black or white, you're a part of the family. We make no issue over a man's color. I just won't tolerate anybody in this organization making it an issue. We respect every man's dignity, black or white."

Over the years, Lombardi demonstrated his commitment to racial equality through his actions as well as his words. When the Packers played an exhibition game in Greensboro, North Carolina, against the Washington Redskins, for instance, a local restaurant owner demanded that all the black players enter and leave through the back door. Incensed, Lombardi ordered that *all* the Packer players enter and leave through the back door. And then, when he lost his fight against a local segregation ordinance that forced all his black players to stay at an all-black Greensboro college, Lombardi called them together while the white players watched from the team bus. "I'll never, absolutely never, put you guys in this situation again," he said apologetically and with tears in his eyes. "If it means we play no games down here, that's the way it will be."

When Emlen Tunnell, the former defensive back whom Vince had lured away from the New York Giants, first arrived in Green Bay, he had difficulty finding a hotel that would accept a black man. So Lombardi got on the telephone and called the top hotel in Green Bay. He told the manager that one of his players needed a room and that he wanted to obtain a special rate. The manager agreed and Vince quickly said: "Oh, yes. The player is a Negro. That won't make any difference, will it?" And then he hung up the phone.

Tunnell later recalled that as far as Green Bay, Wisconsin, was concerned, he had witnessed a major transformation take place. "I saw the community go from one of tolerance of black ballplayers to one where there was, I felt, really no basic difference in how they approached dealing with a Green Bay Packer [black or white]. Vinny turned that whole town around. *He* did it."

Lombardi was proud of that fact—and his overall stance on racial equality. "Of all the years that I've been in football," he said, "never have there ever been any racial or social problems on my team. All things are equal. . . . I've [coached] people from all over the country, and everybody is accepted, regardless of your race, regardless of your social or religious status and beliefs. There are not any barriers. I think these are important things."

Vince's strong feelings on racial equality can be attributed, in part, to his Catholic upbringing and his ongoing religious faith. Although he did not often speak about this aspect of his life, which he deemed very private, he was once overheard at a social event chastising a man who had made a bigoted comment. "How can you, as a good Christian, feel that way?" Vince angrily asked.

Another reason for his adamant position, however, was his personal experience as a victim of prejudice. Willie Davis remembered that he would often go into Lombardi's office, close the door, and have some very personal discussions. "He talked about the parallels of his situation and mine," said Davis. "He felt that because he was Italian he'd been held back for a long time and he said that's the way it was for Negroes now. He talked about all the jobs he applied for and got turned down or never even got answers. [But] he was not bitter when he talked about his past. I think he used it with me to show that he had great empathy for the problems of blacks all over."

Leo Paquin, a friend of Lombardi from his college days, remembered several fights Vince got into because another person called him a derogatory name. One incident occurred when several players were showering after football practice. When a dark-complexioned player entered the shower room, another individual called out, "Hey, come here. Stand alongside Lombardi. I want to see which one of you looks more like a nigger." Even though the guy was larger and heavier, Vince immediately punched him in the face, and a bloody fight ensued for which both men were suspended from the football squad.

Another time, Vince and a friend, Jim Lawlor, had just walked into a sorority dance when a fraternity member blurted out, "Who's the little wop?" "Vince never stopped," recalled Lawlor. "He turned around and as he did his fist came with him and he hit the guy right in the mouth."

Lombardi's personal experience with ethnic prejudice clearly influenced his position when dealing with racial issues. But as a leader, he also realized the divisiveness that might be inflicted on his organization as a result could not be allowed. "Any kind of separatism is bad," he lectured, "in football or anywhere else. . . . We [must] develop a cohesive machine in which the color lines disappear and the various national origins are nonexistent."

In effect, then, when Lombardi took a hard line against racial intolerance, he was removing a potential source of divisiveness on his team. "When a black man and a white man are aiming for the same thing—and working for it together—whether it be a touchdown or increased sales volume for a product," Vince once explained to a group of business people, "they will operate smoothly because the common denominator that is driving them in the same direction becomes so much more important than individual differences."

Oddly enough, though, when it came to distinguishing colors, Vince really was unable to always see a difference. "Not many people knew it, but he was color-blind," Marie Lombardi said of her husband. "He could tell green from red or orange from brown, but he had trouble with shadings, subtleties."

And over the years, many people noted that Lombardi's inability to distinguish shades of gray, or other colors, was a metaphor for his high standards of honesty and integrity. Edward Bennett Williams, owner of the Washington Redskins, for instance, once observed that Vince "saw everything as black and white. He saw a dichotomy between right and wrong; he didn't see twilight areas."

It's no wonder, then, that when that *New York Sports* editor asked a sensitive question about Willie Davis, Vince Lombardi abruptly responded: "You know, I really don't know what color Willie Davis is. And I don't care."

Lombardi Principles

- In dealing with individuals on your team, have no sense of who's black or white.
- Make every member of your team part of a family.
- At your first team meeting, let everybody know that you will not tolerate racial intolerance of any kind.
- Demonstrate your commitment to equality through your actions as well as your words.
- In football or anywhere else, any kind of separatism is bad.
- Removing racial intolerance removes a potential source of divisiveness on your team.
- Develop a cohesive machine in which the color lines disappear and the various national origins are nonexistent.
- Create a common denominator on your team that becomes much more important that any potential individual differences.
- Respect every person's dignity.

A leader must remember that simplicity is the sign of true greatness and meekness is the sign of true strength.

VINCE LOMBARDI

If a man is running down the street with everything you own, you won't let him get away. That's tackling!

VINCE LOMBARDI

9 Keep Things Simple

"You guys are without doubt the dumbest bunch of supposed college graduates I've ever had the misfortune to be associated with in my life!" screamed Vince Lombardi to the offensive squad of the New York Giants. Then he stormed out of the meeting room as the players chuckled in amusement at this display of rage by their new coach.

It was 1954, Lombardi's first training camp with the Giants, and he had been at the blackboard trying to explain his new system of calling "automatics" at the line of scrimmage. "If the quarterback wants to change the play from a 41 to a 49, all he has to do is yell '8' at the line of scrimmage before the snap of the ball," explained Vince. "It can work that way in every instance."

"Jesus Christ!" yelled one player from the back of the room. "Do I have to carry an adding machine with me?"

That's when Lombardi threw down his chalk and stormed out of the room. The squad waited around a few minutes for him to come back, but he didn't return—until the next day.

"All right," he said as he opened the meeting, "for you dummies who can't add or subtract, we're going to make this easier for you. If the quarterback wants to call an audible at the line of scrimmage, he first yells the snap count, say '2,' and then he calls the play number, say '49.' So, he'll yell '2-49,' and the defense still won't know what's going on."

This time the Giant players were impressed with their new coach. He had not only listened to them; he had simplified the new system so they could both easily remember and implement it.

This incident with the New York Giants reinforced Lombardi's conviction that the lessons he conveyed as a leader needed to be uncomplicated and easily understood. And, over the years, he constantly sought to simplify everything he coached.

By the time he took over the Green Bay Packers, he had reduced the game of football, his profession, to essentials and basics. "Football is a simple game," he preached to the Packer players. "It is, first, getting the ball off your own goal line and, second, getting it across our opponent's goal line."

Lombardi described the offense as a series of plays, each "a stepping-stone to where all teams want to go—the end zone." And he not only stressed basic fundamentals by simply stating, "Fundamentals win it," or, "You block and tackle better than the team you're playing and you win," but he specifically described his idea of what "tackling" meant. "If a man is running down the street with everything you own, you won't let him get away," said Vince. "That's tackling!"

He took complex subject matter and conveyed it in an uncomplicated way. Wherever possible, for instance, he simplified his explanations by reducing the subject to "two things." "The defensive secondary has two primary functions," he'd say, "One, to contain or to force the end run, and two, defense against the pass." "Football is two things," he'd stress. "It's blocking and tackling."

When he could not reduce his explanation to "two things," Lomardi would present a visual image for the players to concentrate on. For example, he described the structure of his pass defense as a four-sided pyramid. "The base of that pyramid is the rush of the defensive front four. One side is the practiced patience and the acquired knowledge of the linebackers and defensive backs. Another side is the correct reading of the key offensive players. And the fourth side of our pyramid is the proper playing of the receivers by the defensive backs and linebackers. And that leads us to the apex of the structure, which is the interception,"

Lombardi would conclude. "For it is here where we may turn the game around, maybe even the season."

Packer players marveled at Lombardi's elementary and adroit methods, in general. They called his system "precise" and "beautifully designed." Everything was "logical" or "new" or "exciting." "We didn't have forty plays to run," marveled Jim Taylor. "We had fifteen to twenty."

While simple things can be done with consistent excellence, complex things can only be achieved with sporadic excellence. But Vince Lombardi wanted things done well all the time. So, in effect, by simplifying everything, he increased his odds of team excellence—which meant the Packers would win more games. "We try to make it as uncomplicated as we can," he said, "because I believe that if you block and tackle better than the other team and the breaks are even, you're going to win."

Willie Davis pointed out another key reason that Lombardi left things as uncomplicated as possible. "He liked to establish responsibility on the field," explained Davis. "I think this is why he left things so simple. He wanted to have a situation where he could hold you responsible for what you did or didn't do."

In effect, then, keeping things simple enabled Lombardi to empower his players on the playing field. They weren't encumbered by a lot of rules, by a lot of dos and don'ts. They had the freedom to act on their own under game situations. And Vince would reinforce that idea during his pregame pep talks, reminding his players to "switch their tactics if necessary" or to "adjust accordingly."

And when Lombardi had something to say to his team, everybody listened. Quarterback Zeke Bratkowski remembered that "nobody ever stood to the back or side of him. He moved [so] everybody was in front of him." Players talked about his "dynamic, magnetic force" when addressing the group or, after a speech was over, wanting to "run through a wall for the man." Emlen Tunnell said that even though he was thirty-six years old and thought he had a little sophistication, "when I heard those pep talks, I'd cry and go out and try to kill people. Nobody else could ever do that to me."

Lombardi affected people so profoundly, in part, because of his passion and sincerity. "Everything he said came from way down deep inside," recalled Packer executive Ockie Krueger. And Lombardi seemed always to speak with simple and clear language, using no big words, so people could easily understand him. "It was as if he were teaching the bottom ten percent of the class," remembered Wellington Mara.

Lombardi also made frequent use of stories, anecdotes, and clichés to help get across his point. "I have the feeling that each day Lombardi tried to think of some little story or parable that he might tell that will stick in your mind all week," remembered defensive back Pat Fischer. Bart Starr claimed that Lombardi was "a great slogan man" who would post various quotes in the locker room and then discuss them at team meetings.

"In coaching, you speak in clichés," Lombardi once said. "We're always looking for catchphrases, especially with a connotation of masculinity." Some of the slogans he used were never forgotten by Packer players. And Vince himself said, "I believe every one of them." They included:

"There is no substitute for hard work."

"Confidence is contagious. So is lack of confidence."

"You need fear nothing as long as you are aggressive and keep going."

"The harder you work, the harder it is to surrender."

"Physical toughness will make the opponent weaken and mental toughness will make him crack."

"Make that second effort."

"Run to daylight."

"Success demands singleness of purpose."

"Many run the race in the arena, but one man wins."

Vince Lombardi communicated in simple terms and devised simple strategies because, as his wife, Marie, said, "He was a very simple man." He was straightforward, direct, and, when spoken to, took things as they were said and did not search for double meanings.

Keeping things simple was a core value of Lombardi's leadership philosophy. "I think a leader must remember that simplicity is the sign of true greatness and meekness is the sign of true strength," he said.

Lombardi Principles

- Listen to the members of your team—and then simplify your system so it can be easily remembered and implemented.
- Wherever possible, reduce your explanation of complex matters to two fundamental things.
- For more complicated subjects, present a visual image for the team to concentrate on.
- Simple things can be done with consistent excellence. Complex things can only be achieved with sporadic excellence. Therefore, simplicity increases your chances of winning.
- Don't encumber your players with a lot of rules. Give them the freedom to act on their own under game situations.
- When speaking to your team, never stand with your back or side to them. Position yourself so everybody is in front of you.
- Speak in simple, understandable language—as though you were talking to the bottom 10 percent of your class.
- In coaching, speak in clichés. Always be looking for catch-phrases.
- Simplicity is the sign of true greatness. Meekness is the sign of true strength.

This is not easy, this effort, day after day, week after week, to keep them up, but it is essential. . . .

VINCE LOMBARDI

He'll cuss you early in the week and kiss you late in the week.

JERRY KRAMER,
ON COACH LOMBARDI

Leadership is based on a spiritual quality, the power to inspire. . . .

VINCE LOMBARDI

10   *Constantly Inspire and Motivate*

One year when Vince Lombardi was head football coach at St. Cecilia High School in Englewood, New Jersey, his team had a particularly tough upcoming contest against a larger and more physically talented Brooklyn Prep team. In the locker room before the game, Lombardi related a story to his players about the time Fordham defeated a powerful St. Mary team with the help of a special pill. Head Coach Jim Crowley, he said, had given each football player a pill before the game that made him bigger and stronger. Lombardi told the kids he knew it had worked because he was one of the players who took the pill. "It hardened my muscles and expanded my chest," he said. "Luckily, I was able to obtain some of those pills for you guys." With that, Lombardi pulled out a bottle and, with the aid of a tweezer, slowly and carefully rationed one tablet to each of his players, who swallowed them and then, feeling like supermen, promptly went out and won the football game. Lombardi, however, had made up the whole story, and the pills he had given the kids were harmless placebos.

Another year, the week before a game against the same powerhouse high school, St. Cecilia football players began receiving postcards in the mail that contained insulting and derogatory comments. Each card was signed by an opposing member of the Brooklyn Prep football team. "Naturally, we got all fired up and went out and beat them," said one St. Cecilia player. But a couple of weeks later, everyone learned that Lombardi himself had written the postcards and mailed them from Brooklyn.

From the day he became a football coach with St. Cecilia to the day he stepped down as the premier head coach in professional football, Vince Lombardi was always attuned to the varying moods, feelings, and performances of each member of his team. And depending on the moment at hand, he would do whatever he could to get the most out of his players.

"Week after week, you have to scratch to find some way to keep your own people emotionally up," he said. "The conditions have to dictate what you say. You know, like how the team is playing, what the other team is doing, what position you are in the standings, how many people may be hurt on your team, and so on."

When the Packers were playing well, for instance, he might encourage his men to keep doing what they were doing, or he might say little, hoping not to upset their rhythm. But if he sensed any overconfidence, he would lecture them that they had to "prove themselves all over again every Sunday."

"You have to know what to say," Lombardi noted. "If the team you're playing that week is not as good as you and if you and the players know it, maybe that's the week you don't say too much. [And] there are certain weeks when you feel you are the better football team, and if they just go out and play their game you'll win. And that's the week you say very little, saving what you would have said for another time."

So Lombardi took it game by game, ever cautious not to look too far into the future lest he lose sight of the potential victory at hand. He was focused on the immediate task. And because a key part of leadership itself is about winning the moment, Vince was always perched like an agile cat ready to pounce at any given instant if there was even the slightest hint that his team might come down from its peak level of performance.

After a disappointing defeat on the road, Packer players would find their head coach walking through the plane (on the trip home) ruffling their hair, giving some encouragement, telling jokes, trying to make them laugh. After one particularly tough loss against the Baltimore

Colts, Lombardi even put on a ridiculous Halloween mask and ran up and down the aisle trying to cheer everybody up.

And there were times when Lombardi would post newspaper clippings on the team bulletin board that quoted upcoming opponents—especially if those quotes had the potential to be insulting or infuriating to his team. In 1967, for example, when Green Bay was preparing to play in the Western Conference championship game against the Los Angeles Rams (who had won eight games in a row, including one over the Packers, and carried the best record in the National Football League at 11-1-2), he posted a newspaper article titled "Packer Opponents No Longer in Awe" that contained taunts from some of the confident Rams. The Packers then won the game handily, 28–7, on the way to their third consecutive world championship and second Super Bowl win.

Often Vince would call individuals into his office and ask them for their advice on how to keep the team motivated. He would also urge his veteran players to show some leadership themselves. After an early loss to the Vikings in 1967, for example, Vince assembled his top fourteen veterans. "Frankly, I'm worried," he told them, even though he wasn't worried at all. "I just don't know what the hell to do," he said, even though he knew exactly what needed to be done.

"He kind of put the horse on our shoulders and told us to carry it," remembered Jerry Kramer. "He said it was going to be up to us veterans to bring the new boys along, to get something out of them, and to help him."

Lombardi asked his veterans to take on leadership roles because he knew that people derive inspiration from their involvement. He also realized that when people are involved in the planning, managing, and leading of the organization, they tend to have more pride in their team and its efforts.

And *pride* was something Vince frequently appealed to in members of his team—pride in their profession, pride in their city, pride in their personal performances. "He used to tell us that what made football the greatest profession was that we went out and did our job even if we were hurting," remembered Sonny Jurgensen. "He built [things] up so the thing was you were defending the pride of Green Bay," recalled Willie Davis.

At halftime of one contest against the Detroit Lions, with his team trailing by a score of 21–3, virtually all Lombardi said was: "Men, we are the Green Bay Packers. The Packers have pride." Green Bay came back in the second half to win that game 31–21.

Prior to another contest (with the Los Angeles Rams in '67), Vince made an emotional appeal to his team: "I wish I didn't have to ask you boys to go out there today and do the job," he said. "I wish I could go out and do it myself. Boy, this is one game I'd really like to be playing in. This is a game that you're playing for your pride."

"I saw his leg shaking," remembered Willie Davis. "He was trembling like a leaf."

"If these guys can come into your own backyard and whip you," continued Lombardi, "they'll think they can beat you anywhere, on a street, in an alley, on the corner of Sunset and Vine. You'll have to run from those guys for the rest of your lives."

"By the time we took to that field," said Willie Wood, "every Green Bay Packer was not only going to win that football game; we were going to prove to ourselves our right to be called men."

But for all his inspiring pep talks, his appeals to pride, his psychological tactics, his jokes, and his words of encouragement and praise, Vince Lombardi also cursed, hollered, ranted, raved, threatened, and intimidated his teams. If the Packers weren't progressing to his satisfaction during the week, he might call the squad together and say something like, "You people aren't ready! You've got a lackadaisical attitude. You're going to go out there and get the hell kicked out of you! You're a disgrace!" After one particularly bad practice, Lombardi started screaming at his defensive squad in front of the entire team. "That's the way, defense!" he bellowed. "That's the way! You win one game and you get sloppy. Just stand up and let anybody knock you down. You're going to get knocked down Sunday, you damn fools!" And then he stormed off the field shouting, "Jerks! Jerks! Jerks!" at the top of his lungs.

Many such tirades were staged for effect. But there were times when Lombardi simply lost his temper and got out of control. While he never physically assaulted any member of his team, he did throw helmets and trash cans, slam lockers and doors, and get so red in the face while screaming in anger that sometimes players would cower in his presence.

After one loss, he became so irate that, during a team meeting, he lifted a chair high over tight end Marv Fleming and screamed, "I get so mad at Marvin I'd like to beat him on the head!" Lombardi then lowered the chair to the floor and started swearing and cussing at Fleming, calling him "stupid" and "lazy." Next he turned to the backup tight end, Allen Brown, and chewed him out for letting "a big stupe like [Fleming] beat you out." Brown had not even played in the game against the Colts.

The Packer players also learned that such emotional outbursts from their head coach could take place when they *won* a game if they did not play up to his expectations. Tackle Bob Skoronski recalled casually walking off the field after the Packers had sloppily pummeled the St. Louis Cardinals, 41–14. "Some guy yelled, 'Hey, you'd better get in here,'" said Skoronski. "Lombardi was standing on a chair in the middle of the room screaming. And I thought, *God, I must be in the wrong locker room. I thought we won!*"

Lombardi justified these methods to those who tended to criticize him. "Hell, I can't just sit around and see an error being made and not say anything about it," he remarked. "I like to think I've had some experience in this business, and you don't win when you're making a lot of errors, not the way I tell them. But they've got to be told and told until they get to the point where they don't make them anymore."

But the "way" Lombardi lectured his players—the yelling, screaming, the verbal abusiveness—was resented by some people, and Vince knew it. Still, he felt he had to use such tactics even though, at times, he regretted it. "He would be exhausted and he'd feel terrible about having done it," remembered Edward Bennett Williams. Other times, though, Lombardi would be pleased. "He'd come in and laugh at himself and say, 'Oh, I was mean today,'" remembered former assistant Dave Slattery.

Interestingly enough, many players responded to Lombardi's coercive goading. Fuzzy Thurston once got so furious at Lombardi's charge of malingering and complaining, that he tore the bandages from his injured limbs, screamed, "I'll show that son of a bitch" and played the next preseason game like a wild man, thereby ensuring his position on the starting team. "We were always trying to show him he was wrong," observed Emlen Tunnell. "That was his psyche."

Clearly, some of Lombardi's players were motivated out of pure fear. "You'd better not blow it or it's all over for you," said safety Tom Brown, who once played a game with a dislocated shoulder. "He instilled that in you."

Despite those "whippings," most of the players valued Lombardi's methods because they helped the overall performance of the team. "He whipped us, but we needed whipping," noted Jerry Kramer. "He was a coach who really challenged you," said Willie Davis. "Many times, he was a real big help to us. Football is a game of emotion and the old man excelled at motivation . . . either he got us so mad we wanted to prove something to him or we were fearful of being singled out as the one guy who didn't do the job."

Lombardi purposely and strategically encouraged his players to build up a "competitive animosity" and an "anger" toward upcoming opponents. "To play this game, you must have that fire in you," he told a writer for *Look* magazine, "and there is nothing that stokes that fire like hate. I'm sorry, but that is the truth."

After Lombardi's statement appeared in the magazine and he came under a good deal of criticism, Vince qualified himself a bit. "Well, maybe *hate* was a little strong," he responded. "When I say 'hate,' I don't mean I wish anybody any physical harm. But I do have to build up an emotion before a game to do a good job. If I go out there feeling just fine about everything and everybody, I'm not going to do the job I should do. Besides, the hatred vanishes as soon as the game ends."

Whether it was with hate or love, Vince Lombardi was constantly trying to motivate and inspire. And his football players noticed clear patterns in their coach's methods. He would be critical on Tuesdays and Wednesdays. But beginning on Thursdays, he would compliment them because he didn't want any sulking just before a game. "He'll cuss you early in the week and kiss you late in the week," said Jerry Kramer. "Each day he sells the team," Pat Fischer observed. "He's leading up to the right moment to clinch the sale, and that's supposed to be on Sunday. That's the day we buy. He always tried to close the sale on Sunday. Sometimes he does and sometimes he doesn't. It's hard to sell forty men week after week."

And Vince agreed. "This is not easy, this effort, day after day, week after week, to keep them up," he said, "but it is essential. . . ." "Leadership is based on a spiritual quality," he also said, "the power to inspire, the power to inspire others to follow. [And] a leader is judged in terms of what others do to obtain the results that he is placed there to get."

So Lombardi was forever on top of his players. And whether it was shocking them after a couple of grueling weeks of preparation with a statement like, "Okay, fellas, this is it! There's no tomorrow! This is really the start of the big push," or hammering them with verbal abuse, Vince never let up, not even for a moment.

This ongoing effort required a tremendous will and discipline on Lombardi's part. He had to be in just the right frame of mind when he was in front of his team. And because Vince was a congenial person by nature, it often took him a good deal of preparation to work himself up into a rage. "I've got to chew them out tomorrow," he once said to Norb Hecker. "I know what I'll do. I'll get up early in the morning and have a fight with Marie. Then I'll really bury that ball club. I'll be ready to yell all day."

There was one morning, however, when Lombardi had not properly prepared himself. As he cheerily strode into the office, he suddenly realized his mood was all wrong for what he had to do that particular day. So he went into the bathroom, looked at himself in the mirror, and slapped his face a couple of times. "Vince, you're not supposed to be so happy!" he said. "You've got to get it up and get it going!" Then, as he walked out onto the football field, he said to Phil Bengtson, "I'm just going to give these guys complete hell today—no matter what happens. Because today is going to be one of those days."

Lombardi Principles

- Always stay attuned to the varying moods, feelings, and performances of each member of your team.
- Week after week, you have to scratch to find some way to keep your own people emotionally up.
- The conditions have to dictate what you say—or don't say.
- A key part of leadership is that winning the moment.
- Ask your veteran players to assume a leadership role.
- People derive inspiration from their involvement.
- Appeal to a person's sense of pride.
- When you see an error being made, don't just sit around and not say anything about it. People have got to be told and told until they don't make errors anymore.
- At times, get your players angry so they'll be motivated to show you that you're wrong.
- Leadership is based on a spiritual quality, the power to inspire.
- A leader is judged in terms of what others do to obtain the results that he is placed there to get.

On December 31, 1961, the Packers hosted the first NFL championship game ever played in Green Bay, Wisconsin. They had cruised through the regular season with an 11–3 record and had twelve players named All-Pro. Their opponent was a tough New York Giant squad replete with stars like legendary quarterback Y. A. Tittle, standout wide receiver Dale Shofner, leading linebacker Sam Huff, and a formidable defensive line known as the "Fearsome Foursome." The Giants were clearly a stronger team than the previous year, when they defeated Green Bay to take the NFL crown.

In preparation for the previous year's game, Vince Lombardi held his team practices indoors to protect his players from the harsh outside elements. But this year, with subfreezing temperatures hovering near zero, all practices the week before the big game were held outdoors. For one session, the outside temperature was minus ten degrees Fahrenheit. Lombardi dressed himself in a large overcoat, gloves, and a red stocking mask over his face (with holes for eyes, nose, and mouth). As steam gusted from every word he spoke and every breath he took, Lombardi stood on the back of a blocking sled exhorting his players to "hit me hard" and "stop feeling sorry for yourselves."

During the championship game, Green Bay punted only once—on their opening possession. Bart Starr threw for three touchdowns, had no interceptions, and completed 58.8 percent of his passes. Paul Hornung scored a record nineteen points (one rushing touchdown, three field goals, and four extra points). The Packer defense had four interceptions and a fumble recovery. They sacked Tittle twice behind the line of scrimmage and allowed him only six completed passes—three to Shofner. The score was 24–0 at the half, and when the final gun sounded Green Bay had won the NFL championship in a stunning 37–0 shutout.

In the Packer locker room after the game, Vince Lombardi wiped tears from underneath his glasses. "Today, you were the greatest team in the history of the National Football League," he told them. "And I mean it."

In the Giant locker room, standout tackle Greg Larson sat with his head down talking to a reporter. "It was the most awesome thing I've ever been involved in," said Larson. "We had no way to stop them. They were like wild men."

PART III
Routine

We may not know any more about football than most of the other coaches in the league, but we can put everything we know together so it makes good basic sense and then drill-drill-drill it into them.

VINCE LOMBARDI,
TO HIS ASSISTANT COACHES

It could be that our leaders no longer understand the relationship between themselves and the people they lead. That is, while most shout to be independent, at the same time wish to be dependent, and while most shout to assert themselves, at the same time wish to be told what to do.

VINCE LOMBARDI

The leader must be willing to use [authority]. His leadership is then based on truth and character.

VINCE LOMBARDI

11 Take Charge

When Vince Lombardi first met with the Green Bay Packers' board of directors in 1959, he was straightforward and frank. "I want it understood that I'm in complete command," he said. "I expect full cooperation from you people, and you will get full cooperation from me in return. You have my confidence, and I want yours."

Ten years later, in 1969 and just a few weeks after he took over the helm of the Washington Redskins, Lombardi was equally frank with owner Edward Bennett Williams after Williams mentioned that quarterback Sonny Jurgensen had come into his office for a talk. "Wait a minute," exploded Lombardi. "I want you to remember one damn thing. If you ever talk to the ballplayers or disrupt anything I'm trying to do here, you can find yourself a new coach! I'm the one who's coach. I don't want you to talk to anybody!"

Williams's private reaction was much the same as that of the Packers' board members a decade before. "I craved someone to take charge," marveled Williams.

And take charge Lombardi did—from his very first day of practice when he gathered all the Green Bay Packers together and told them the way things were going to be. He asserted that he was the head coach, that he was running the show, that he was in charge. He also said he was "tough as nails," that he "would trade anyone at the drop of a hat," and that they could "stay here and pay the price for winning" or "get the hell out."

Most of the players reacted with dismay at his tough opening remarks. But some were extremely impressed. *Holy cow*, thought Bart Starr, *where have you been all my life?* Others, like Forrest Gregg, just took it for what it was. "From the first day you came to camp, you knew who the boss was," said Gregg. "You knew who you had to answer to and who you had to satisfy as a football player."

Interestingly enough, Lombardi himself had some major concerns about making that first speech. Immediately afterward he called veteran Max McGee into his office and revealed that he was scared to death everybody was going to walk out. "I don't know what's going to happen," Lombardi told McGee, "but if they stay, I've got them."

Lombardi may have chosen McGee to confide in because he was one of two players with whom the coach had already established his authority. Both McGee and running back Howie Ferguson had arrived at camp two days early—not to start working out but to relax and get in a couple of free meals. The first night, they ate dinner in the team dining room, then visited a few nightclubs, and stayed out late. The next morning, as the two headed to breakfast, their new head coach called them into his office.

"You guys start working today!" shouted Lombardi. "And you start keeping curfew today! As far as I'm concerned, when you ate a meal here yesterday, you became part of this camp. Therefore, you abide by all my rules!"

"What the hell are you talking about?" protested Ferguson. "We don't have to report for two more days."

"Listen, mister," roared Lombardi, "you get your ass out there on the field—or get your ass out of here!"

McGee later recalled that Ferguson and Lombardi began screaming at each other while he just sat there in stunned silence. "You know, you meet a guy for the first time," said McGee, "and he starts chewing your ass out, yelling and hollering. I was thinking maybe I ought to go somewhere else."

But McGee and Ferguson both stayed—as did the rest of the squad. And they all found out very quickly that "all my rules," as Lombardi phrased it, were really not all that bad. Among them were standard things like: everybody present and paying attention at every meeting, including meals and practices; everybody on time; curfews adhered to; certain nightclubs off-limits. But there were also some quirky things Vince insisted upon. For example, when in a restaurant or pub, nobody was allowed to belly up to a bar. Rather, they had to sit at a table or a booth. "One thing I won't stand for," he said, "is a player standing at a public bar. I don't care if he's drinking ginger ale and talking to a friend. It just doesn't look good if a fan sees him in the place."

To the team, Vince clearly explained his rules and the penalties for each infraction (which were usually fines). But when Vince first took over a team, many players tried to take advantage of him or, at the very least, test his limits. As offensive coach for the New York Giants, for instance, Lombardi found himself dealing with professional football players for the first time. Seasoned pros like Kyle Rote, Charlie Conerly, and Frank Gifford told their new coach they wanted to stay out of preseason games so they could study the opposition. At first, Lombardi deferred to them by *asking* them if they wanted to go into games. After a while, though, he began *ordering* them to "get in there"—and they complied. "We realized he'd caught up with us," recalled Rote.

By the time Lombardi got to the Packers, however, he was more seasoned in dealing with professionals and did not put up with any nonsense. Bart Starr remembered, for example, how in early practices several players tried to cheat during the grass drills (where players run in place, dive on their bellies, jump back up on their feet, etc.). "There were some who halfway through would just sort of peel off and not do them—or skip one or two," said Starr. "Boy, the first time [Lombardi] caught them doing that, he just made everybody do more. . . . So there wasn't too much testing after a while."

Lombardi also cut several players in a most public way. A veteran fullback, Ray McDonald, had been missing assignments and not adjusting well to the new regime. And when he showed up late for a practice, Lombardi had had enough—and he cut McDonald on the spot. "That really put the fear in a lot of people," recalled lineman Ray Schoenke.

Another time, a player kept falling asleep during team meetings and Lombardi, who had been watching closely, finally walked over to the player, picked up his playbook, and said: "Any man who can't stay awake in one of the most important meetings we have—the rules meet-ing, where you can learn something—why, he doesn't belong with the Packers."

"Coach Lombardi told this guy to get out of the room, to get dressed and go home," remembered Mark Duncan. "He cut the guy right there in front of the entire team."

Then there was the famous story of seven-time All-Pro center Jim Ringo. According to legend, in 1964 Ringo sent his agent in to negotiate a better contract with Lombardi, who was, of course, general manager of the Packers as well as head coach. "Excuse me for a moment," said Lombardi, who then walked out of the room. Five minutes later, he returned and said: "I'm afraid you have come to the wrong city to dis-cuss Mr. James Ringo's contract. Mr. James Ringo is now the property of the Philadelphia Eagles."

Word got around the Packer organization that when Lombardi left the room he immediately telephoned the general manager of the Philadelphia Eagles and arranged the trade. "To hell with Ringo and his agent!" Lombardi was supposed to have shouted. "Let's show them who's boss here."

But the truth is that Ringo had asked Lombardi to be traded to the Eagles so he could be closer to his home in Pennsylvania. Vince had arranged for it ahead of time and kept the whole thing quiet. But when he found out how the story had been twisted, rather than trying to set the record straight, Lombardi actually perpetuated the myth.

"Yeah, yeah, yeah!" he exclaimed to a reporter when asked about agents and excessive financial demands from players. "They both get hustled out of my office in a hurry. And the one with the ultimatum, if he does not relent, gets traded!"

To a close friend, however, Vince admitted that the rumor was not true. "Hell, no, the trade didn't take place in five minutes," he said. "That's no way to general-manage a football team." And yet, because the myth endured, from that day forward, people rarely challenged him during contract negotiations.

Overall, Lombardi's philosophy was that a leader had to both respect and exude authority. "The leader must be willing to use [authority]," he stated. "His leadership is then based on truth and character."

And throughout his career, Vince thought deeply about the relation-ships between leaders and followers—about psychological, philosophi-cal, and practical ideas regarding human nature and human interactions.

During a speech to a large business group, he reflected on this thinking. "Maybe we have so long ridiculed authority in the family and discipline in education and decency in conduct and law in the state," he said, "that the freedom we fought so hard for has brought us close to chaos. And it could be that our leaders no longer understand the relationship between themselves and the people they lead. That is, while most shout to be independent, at the same time wish to be dependent, and while most shout to assert themselves, at the same time wish to be told what to do."

At least one Green Bay Packer confirmed Lombardi's perceptive observation. Center Bill Curry noted that he and many of the players had something of a "love-hate" relationship with their head coach. "He used his ability to manipulate you, to make you do whatever he wanted you to do," said Curry. "It was somehow demeaning, and yet at the same time, it was exhilarating to be a part of all this because you knew that you were in the presence of greatness."

As a leader, Vince Lombardi was both serious and self-confident—serious in his disposition toward the players on his team, self-confident in his personal demeanor. And that self-confidence, Lombardi believed, was innate. "I've never been apprehensive in my life," he said. "You've got to do things according to your own personality, and being apprehensive isn't a part of mine." Leaders, he believed, had to have "an inclination, a commitment, a willingness to command." And they also had to maintain a certain amount of distance between them and the people in their organization. When Lombardi was assistant coach with the New York Giants, for instance, the players affectionately called him Vinny. But when he went to the Packers as head coach and general manager, he was always referred to as Coach, Coach Lombardi, or Mr. Lombardi. Now that he had the top position, as he said to a friend, he could "no longer be one of the boys."

Both Packer players and assistant coaches noted Lombardi's seriousness in keeping them at an arm's length. "I've known him sixteen years now, and I've never really socialized with him," said Coach Bill Austin. "I just couldn't get close to him personally," lamented guard Fuzzy Thurston.

The distance Lombardi kept between himself and the members of his team was part of his leadership plan. By strategic design, Vince Lombardi was openly authoritarian. "No one *ever* challenged his authority," said one player. "He was the absolute dictator." "He rules," noted Jerry Kramer. "You do it his way or you don't do it at all."

"The voice, like the personality, had just the most indescribable intensity," remembered center Bill Curry. "His was a presence that you could sense. It motivated people to perform. It wasn't malevolent. It scared. It was unique. He could elicit the damnedest, deepest reaction from you. He was a walking, living, breathing piece of motivation all the time; he never shut off, never turned off."

Lombardi's reason for such authoritarian behavior was pure and simple. He used his power and his authority to *motivate* people.

And motivate them he did. "When Lombardi turns to us in the locker room and tells us to sit down," said one player, "I don't even look for a chair." "If he told me to run into the stands and start selling programs, I wouldn't question it," said Paul Hornung. "When Lombardi tells you to go to hell," quipped receiver Gary Knaflec, "you look forward to the trip."

Defensive tackle Henry Jordan once even amusingly hinted that Lombardi's force of will was supernatural. "One morning, we went out to the stadium, and it was pouring down rain," related Jordan to a writer. "I just took one look at the sky, and I knew it was gonna rain all day. Lombardi was pretty unhappy, walking around, wringing his hands, looking disgusted with the weather. Finally, he cut out pacing and looked up at the heavens and shouted, 'Stop raining! Stop raining!' And there was a huge clap of thunder and a flash of lightning—and the rain stopped. I'm a hard-shelled Methodist," concluded Jordan, "but I've been eating fish every Friday since then."

Even if Lombardi's authoritative personality was not mystical, it was clearly felt by any creature that crossed his path—as this story from Bill Curry illustrates:

> One day while we were practicing, a little dog came out and started prancing around the practice field. Nobody could concentrate because he was running in and out between people's legs. Just a cute little setter dog. Guys were trying to shoo him away—"Go! Go!"—and he'd scamper off and then run back, wagging his tail and having a good time.
>
> Lombardi was about sixty yards away at the other end of the field, and suddenly his voice came booming from down there: "*Get the hell off the field!*"
>
> I swear I saw this happen. The dog tucked his tail between his legs, and the last time we saw him he was rounding a corner two blocks away from the field.

Lombardi Principles

- Expect full cooperation from your superiors, and give full cooperation in return.
- Immediately establish your authority with the members of your team.
- Set standard rules that everybody can live with—and enforce them evenhandedly.
- Remember that people will test your limits when you first start out.
- Firing some people in front of the rest of the group will clearly establish that you are the boss.
- Public disregard for the rules needs to be dealt with publicly.
- As a leader, be willing to use authority. Your leadership is then based on truth and character.
- Remember, if you're going to exercise authority, you've got to respect it.
- While most people shout to be independent, they also wish to be dependent.
- Be serious in your disposition toward members of your team and self-confident in your personal demeanor.
- As a leader, you must have an inclination, a commitment, a willingness to command.
- Keep the members of your team at arm's length.
- Be openly authoritarian. Use your power and authority to motivate people.

They call it coaching, but it is teaching. You do not just tell them it is so. You show them the reasons why it is so and then you repeat and repeat until they are convinced, until they know.

VINCE LOMBARDI

You gotta seal off the linebacker! You gotta seal off the linebacker! You gotta seal off the linebacker! Run it again.

VINCE LOMBARDI,
DURING PRACTICE

When you went in to look at the film on Tuesday, you sweated blood.

FORREST GREGG,
TACKLE, GREEN BAY PACKERS

12   *Learn, Teach, Practice*

In the middle of West Point's very first spring football practice in 1949, Army head coach Earl (Red) Blaik called his new assistant coach for the offense, Vince Lombardi, away from the players to discuss a couple of key points. As the two stood together on the sidelines, Lombardi noticed out of the corner of his eye that a running back had run in the wrong direction while practicing a play. Abruptly turning away from Blaik, Lombardi threw his hat to the ground and ran onto the field toward the player spewing forth obscenities in a vile rebuke.

Shocked, Coach Blaik yelled for Lombardi to come back. "Vince! Vince!" he called out.

When Lombardi heard his boss's voice, he immediately quieted down and ran back to Blaik, who calmly explained that he knew how passionate and determined to succeed Lombardi was. "But, Vince," Blaik concluded, "we don't coach that way at West Point."

"Yes, sir," came the submissive reply.

And Red Blaik recalled years later that that was the one and only time he ever had to admonish Vince Lombardi.

This early confrontation with one of his mentors vividly indicates two important points about Lombardi. First, he had a tremendous respect for authority. When Blaik spoke, Vince shut up and said, "Yes, sir." Second, the fact that Blaik never had to rebuke Vince again indicates a genuine willingness and capacity to learn.

Collectively, mentors such as Harry Kane, Jim Crowley, Frank Leahy, and Red Blaik molded Lombardi's entire approach to coaching, having had a direct impact not only on his detailed knowledge of football but also on such principles as: *firm discipline, a hard work ethic, insisting that players be gentlemen, stressing fundamentals, repetition through practice*, and *an emphasis on winning*. So by the time he reached the rank of head coach in professional football, Lombardi had gained a great deal of knowledge from Red Blaik and several other formidable coaches under whom he had worked during his formative years. Vince had perfected his ability to organize, discipline, and inspire a team. And, interestingly enough, he implemented his acquired wisdom by employing all the skills of a world-class teacher.

He taught players to *think for themselves* and gave them *reasons why* something was being done. "Lombardi never put in a play before he explained to everyone why that play was put in, why it was to be run a certain way, and what the defense would do," recalled Tom Miller, the Packers' public relations director.

He *injected enthusiasm and passion* into his teaching. "He could romance a block to the point where the guy who was going to do it really thought he enjoyed this thing," said Fuzzy Thurston.

He *made football enjoyable*. "Coach Lombardi made playing the game fun," said Bart Starr.

And Lombardi *did not assume everybody already knew everything*. In fact, he asked his players to wipe the slate clean and start fresh in their thinking. "He told us to forget everything," said Max McGee, "to scrap it all; that we were going back to basics and fundamentals." That turned out to make all the difference in the world to players who had previously been struggling. Before Lombardi took over at Green Bay, for instance, many of the Packer players were uneducated in key areas of football. "Hell, before Vince got there, even our quarterbacks didn't know what a zone was," remembered Paul Hornung. "We just called some kind of

pass on third down, and that was it. If it went incomplete, we just figured it was a bad pass. We didn't know there was a *reason* it went incomplete."

Sonny Jurgensen said virtually the same thing a decade later when
Lombardi took over the Washington Redskins. "[Before Lombardi], I
was struggling every week," recalled Jurgensen. "It was always second
and eight. We were always making up plays in the huddle. . . . I used to
force the ball, throw no matter what the coverage was. 'We don't force
the ball,' he said—and he *showed me* what he meant."

At the beginning of each season, Lombardi almost always focused on
basic principles. "The development of all talent is founded on the fundamentals," he said. "Fundamentals win it." And during the season,
when his team might be struggling, he would *get back* to basics. During
his first year with Green Bay, for example, after the Packers lost five
games in a row, Lombardi pulled the team together for a stern talking-
to. "You forgot every basic fundamental about this game," he lectured.
"We are going to have to start all over again, from scratch." Then he
picked up a ball and said: "Gentlemen, the basics. *This* is a football!"

At that point, the tension in the room was high. Everybody had just
been chewed out and Max McGee, ever the one to help Lombardi move
things along, called out from the back of the room, "Hold on a minute,
Coach! You're going too fast!"

Lombardi was also such a perfectionist that he insisted his players
rehearse their roles down to the smallest detail. "So much of teaching is
repetition," he said. "I believe a coach must be a pedagogue. He has to
pound the lessons into the players by rote, the same way you teach
pupils in the classroom. . . . Every game boils down to doing the things
you do best and doing them over and over and over again."

Former players remember that practices were filled with Lombardi
admonishments, such as: "You gotta seal off the linebacker! You gotta
seal off the linebacker! You gotta seal off the linebacker! Run it again!"
or, "This is the 26 power play, 26 power play. Do you have that? The
right guard must pull back, must pull back. The right guard must pull
back. The first step is back. Got that? The first step is back."

Predictably, those who picked up things quickly became frustrated
with their coach's constant repetition of instructions. "He drove us
mad!" commented Frank Gifford. But Lombardi persisted, citing one of
his teaching maxims. "In the classroom, you can't travel faster than your
slowest pupil," he said. "[Lombardi] pays such meticulous attention to

detail," recalled Jerry Kramer, "[that] he makes us execute the same plays over and over, a hundred times, two hundred times, until we do every little thing right automatically. He works to make the kickoff-return team perfect, the punt-return team perfect, the field-goal team perfect. He ignores nothing. Technique, technique, technique, over and over and over, until we feel like we're going crazy. But we win."

Lombardi, however, did not apologize for his ongoing redundancy. In fact, he pointed out to his assistant coaches that it was one of their keys to success. "We may not know any more about football than most of the other coaches in the league," he told them, "but we can put everything we know together so it makes good basic sense and then drill-drill-drill it into them."

Of course, Lombardi's main forum for teaching his players technique was football practice, which, as he said, "must be perfectly organized, efficient, and precise." But "practice" wasn't limited to the playing field. It was a week-long, intense process that involved classroom study, systematic film analysis, blackboard discussions, postmortem reviews, precision drilling, game simulations, and individual player grading. "Lombardi would drive us all week until there was nothing that could be unexpected," remembered Bart Starr, "and the playing on Sunday would be the easiest part of the week."

The week's work began on Monday, the day after games. While the players took a breather, Vince and his coaches would watch film from early in the morning until late in the evening. Their routine first involved reviewing the previous day's game. Then they would split up and offensive coaches would watch only defensive plays and defensive coaches would watch only offensive plays. Then they'd get back together and meticulously study their upcoming opponent. Lombardi once explained the kind of detail he and his coaches considered in preparing for a new adversary: "We record the position of the ball on the field, the down and yardage, as well as the formation and the defense, on each play. In this way we build up our whole picture of their defensive preferences, what defenses they use under what situations, so that on Wednesday, we will be able to sit down with our offensive team and say that, in a certain situation, the other people can be expected to be in a certain defense eighty-five or ninety-five percent of the time."

For the players, Tuesday morning was the toughest day of the week because Coach Lombardi personally critiqued their Sunday performances—on film in front of the entire team. "If you didn't play well, you heard from Vince," remembered Forrest Gregg. "When you went in to look at the film on Tuesday, you sweated blood."

During these film sessions, Lombardi both complimented and hammered the players. If one of them executed a block perfectly, it was noted: "Good job! You had a helluva ball game." But if a player's foot was a few inches from where it should be, he was chewed out. "That's God-awful, mister. You stink! Just plain stupidity!"

"Every detail of every single play you were under a microscope," remembered Bill Curry. "You might think he'd miss you on a play, but no, after the eighth time he'd run the play, out would come our name and he'd show everyone what a donkey you were." Jerry Kramer remembered being the victim of one particularly humiliating film session. "I especially didn't enjoy the opening scene," remarked Kramer. "The movie began with that 42-trap play, the one in which I missed the Steeler right end. I thought it was a pretty terrible way to start a movie but, apparently, Vince didn't agree with me. He liked that scene so much he showed it to us nineteen times, and nineteen times I saw myself miss that block. The next time we run a 42-trap, I suspect I'll block a little better."

To Lombardi, this was all part of an essential "postmortem" process that involved recording every detail about the previous game. Mistakes had to be corrected immediately, before they could be overlooked or forgotten. "All learning is trial and error," he said. "The negative experiences do not *inhibit* but rather *contribute* to the learning process. . . . Errors, mistakes, and humiliations are all necessary steps in the learning process. [But] once they have served their purpose, they should be forgotten. If we constantly dwell upon the errors, then the error or failure becomes the goal."

During the week, part of each afternoon was reserved for field practices—which were well planned, meticulously organized, and brief. While many coaches practiced for three hours or more, Lombardi's practices lasted only 75–90 minutes. But they were an intense, flowing, and crisp 75–90 minutes, with no lost time or wasted effort. And there was always variation because, as Lombardi said, "If I get bored coaching the same thing over and over, they are going to get bored learning it."

Each session began with calisthenics and other intense exercises. Then the group moved on to different drills spaced at short intervals. Some were customized for upcoming opponents. Sometimes there was rehearsal of an innovative or trick play. And frequently Vince set up "game simulation" drills by saying something like: "Okay, opponents lead, 7–6, ball on our own 20, less than two minutes to go, offense has to drive 80 yards for a touchdown, less for a field goal; let's go!"

There was one thing that never varied, however. For every practice, Vince was always on the field with his team—right in the middle of the action. He was usually saying things like: "Give me the ball. Here's how you do it"; or he was standing on the back of the blocking sled shouting: "Drive! Drive! Drive! Block! Block! Block!" Furthermore, Lombardi's concentration was unwavering. "Don't bother me now," he would say to anybody who tried to distract him. "Practice doesn't make perfect," he lectured. "*Perfect* practice makes perfect."

Vince also made it a point to hold casual film sessions with his quarterbacks every Wednesday, Thursday, and Friday morning. These informal meetings were designed to refine Sunday's game plan and build strong relationships with his field leaders. Bart Starr described them as more of a discussion between "father and son than lecturer and listener."

And every Friday, the Packers had what Vince termed an *honors assembly*. During this team gathering, the coaches presented awards (based on an individual grading system) that often included small monetary prizes. While some players discounted the ceremony, most took it seriously—especially when they received high or low grades. A high mark earned respect from others. But nobody wanted a low grade because it was embarrassing. Either way, the award and grading system was an effective motivator with respect to pride and performance. "He gave you that five or ten in cash," remembered Packer wide receiver Gary Knafelc, "and when he did that it meant more than anything."

Overall, Vince Lombardi's week-long practice routine was extraordinarily effective in getting his team ready for their next opponent. "The heart of his system was preparation," noted Bart Starr. "He prepared us beautifully for every game, for every eventuality. Nothing was left to chance." Starr also pointed out that Lombardi's system gave him tremendous self-confidence. "I was positive that I would never face a situation I wasn't equipped to handle," he said. And that was exactly how Lombardi meant for it to be. "The man who is trained to his peak capacity will gain confidence," he said. "This is a team that has been built on confidence."

Vince Lombardi's entire system—from film analysis to confidence building—centered around the concept of *teaching* people what to do, as opposed to *mandating* what they do. "They call it coaching, but it is teaching," he explained. "You do not just tell them it is so. You show them the reasons why it is so and then you repeat and repeat until they are convinced, until they know."

And the players clearly recognized and appreciated their coach's approach. Gary Knafelc called Lombardi "the best teacher I ever had." "He was able to see the gap between where we were and what we could become—both as football players and as people," said Jerry Kramer. "And he felt it was his God-given responsibility to close that gap." Lineman Robert Haas insisted that "there was love involved in that kind of teaching."

Marie Lombardi explained that her husband always tried to help people learn and get better. "When Vin gets one he thinks can be a real good ballplayer . . . , he will just open a hole in that boy's head and pour everything he knows into it." Furthermore, it didn't seem to matter to Lombardi whether he was dealing with an adult or a kid.

One morning before going to the office, Lombardi stopped for breakfast at a nearby restaurant and ordered pancakes. But when his meal arrived, he had to send it back because the pancakes were not cooked all the way through. The waitress apologized to Vince and explained that a thirteen-year-old boy, who was trying to learn, had prepared them. And what happened next was never forgotten by that young man. "Coach Lombardi came into the kitchen," he explained years later, "and proceeded to give me a gentle lesson in the proper way of making a flapjack."

Lombardi Principles

- Have respect for authority and a genuine willingness to learn.
- Teach people to think for themselves. Give them reasons why. Inject enthusiasm and passion into your organization. Make it fun. And do not assume everybody knows everything.
- Remember that all talent is founded on fundamentals and that fundamentals win it.
- Every game boils down to doing the things you do best and doing them over and over and over again.
- You can't travel faster than your slowest pupil.
- All practice sessions should be perfectly organized, efficient, and precise.
- Initiate a "postmortem" process. Remember that all learning is trial and error—and that negative experiences do not *inhibit* but rather *contribute* to the learning process.
- If you get bored coaching the same thing over and over, then people are going to get bored learning it.
- Always be on the field with your team—right in the middle of the action.
- Convene casual sessions with your field leaders. It helps to build stronger relationships.
- The man who is trained to his peak capacity will gain confidence.
- People learn by example and explanation.
- When you see the gap between what people are and what they can become, do everything you can to help close it.

Mental toughness is Spartanism with its qualities of sacrifice and self-denial, dedication, fearlessness, and love. [It] is a state of mind. You might call it "character in action."

VINCE LOMBARDI

Drag him off the field and let's get on with the scrimmage!

VINCE LOMBARDI

Fatigue makes cowards of us all.

VINCE LOMBARDI

13   Focus on Physical Fitness, Discipline, and Mental Toughness

"WHAT IS THIS, AN EMERGENCY CASUALTY WARD?!" yelled Lombardi as he walked into the crowded Packer training room.

It was the morning after his very first practice at Green Bay and about twenty players (more than half the team) were sitting around waiting for "diathermy or the whirlpool or a rubdown," as Vince recalled it. "And I blew my stack!"

"Now, get this straight," he said to the players. "When you're hurt, you have every right to be here. BUT THIS IS DISGRACEFUL! I have *no patience* for the small hurts that are bothering most of you. You're going to have to *live* with small hurts, *play* with small hurts, if you're going to play for *me*."

Everybody, veterans and rookies alike, was going to have to prove himself worthy of playing for the Green Bay Packers, Lombardi told the players at the first team meeting. "There is nobody big enough to think he's got the team made," he said. "Trains and planes are going in and coming out of Green Bay every day, and [you could] be on one of them.

I won't." He also promised to work them "like you've never been worked before." "I'm going to push and drive, drive and push," he said. "If you don't think you're a winner, you don't belong here."

And work the players he did—until some of them literally dropped. No one was spared. "He treated us all the same," noted tackle Henry Jordan, "like dogs."

Nearly everyone who experienced it confirmed that Lombardi's conditioning regime was the toughest they ever had to endure from any coach. It began with an incredible "warm-up" calisthenics period that included, as Bill Curry said, "not *fifteen* side-straddle hops, but a *hundred*." Then Lombardi would announce (often with a wry grin on his face) that it was time for the grass drill. A sportswriter for the *New York Post* once wrote about this grueling drill, which Vince directed in a drill-sergeant manner:

> "C'mon, lift those legs, lift 'em. Higher, higher." Suddenly he yells, "Front!" and the players . . . flop on their bellies and as soon as they do, even while they are falling, Lombardi shouts, "Up!" and they must leap to their feet, running, running, faster, higher. "Front!" and they are down. "Back!" and they roll over on their backs. "Up!" Run. "Front!" Down. "Up!" Over and over, always that raucous voice, nagging, urging, demanding ever more from rebelling lungs and legs. "Move those damn legs. This is the worst-looking thing I ever saw. You're supposed to be moving those legs. Front! Up! C'mon, Caffey, move your legs. Keep them moving. C'mon, Willie Davis, you told me you were in shape. Front! Up! C'mon, Crenshaw, get up. It takes you an hour to get up. Faster. Move those legs. Dammit, what the hell's the matter with you guys? You got a lot of dog in you. You're dogs, I tell you. A bunch of dogs. Let's move. Front! Up! For the love of Pete, Crenshaw, you're fat. Ten bucks a day for every pound you don't lose. Crenshaw! It's going to cost you ten bucks a day. Lift those legs!"

The grass drill was immediately followed by 250-yard wind sprints. "When everybody was just literally staggering," recalled Bill Curry, "we'd sprint around the goal post and back to the far end of the field. And you had to *sprint.*"

"Run! Run!" Lombardi would yell at the players. "If you want to walk, you don't belong here!"

During the grass drill and sprints, some players would "drop to one knee and just gasp and pant" or "fall to the ground and not be able to get up." Others would simply pass out. Some were hospitalized. Veteran Redskin guard Vince Promuto called it "the worst thing I've ever been through." And yet, as Phil Bengtson noted, "Nobody vomited after a couple of days." Then fat started to burn off and weights began to drop dramatically. And within a few weeks, most of the players were in the best physical condition of their careers. And of course, collectively, the entire *team* was in the best physical condition it had ever been in.

Lombardi's philosophy was simple: Any player who was not in tip-top condition would not be able to give 100 percent. That's what he believed and that's what he drove his players to believe. He not only ran them until they dropped; he also told them *why* he was running them during the heat of the workouts. "If you quit now, during these work-outs, you'll quit in the middle of the season in a game," Jerry Kramer remembered Lombardi saying. "Once you learn to quit, it becomes a habit. . . . You're preparing yourself mentally. It's tough now, but when the other team quits in the fourth quarter and you're still strong, you'll thank me."

Furthermore, Lombardi constantly lectured the players between workouts that "good physical condition was vital to success" and that it was "smart to get in shape." "You've got to keep yourself in prime phys-ical condition, because fatigue makes cowards of us all," he'd tell them. "When you're tired, you rationalize. You make excuses in your mind. You say, 'I'm too tired; I'm bushed; I can't do this; I'll loaf.' Then you're a coward. . . . The harder you work, the harder it is to surrender."

But Henry Jordan believed that there was another key reason for Lombardi's intense physical regime. "[He] ran you and ran you and ran you, but I don't think it was so much for conditioning as for discipline," speculated Jordan.

Discipline to Vince Lombardi clearly meant adherence to a tough, intense physical program. But it also meant the players had to do *what* they were supposed to do *when* they were supposed to do it. And it meant they had to live by the rules, *his* rules. If he was able to implement it properly, he believed, then discipline *off the field* would lead to disci-pline *on the field* during a game. "In a game like football," he said, "where you have very little time to decide what you are going to do, you have to react almost instinctively, naturally. Without perfect discipline, [football] is nothing, absolutely nothing."

Basically, the bottom line for Vince Lombardi was winning ball games and, as he said: "Winning is gained through discipline." Accordingly, from the first day of training camp, he laid out the ground rules covering behavior and conduct for all members of the Green Bay Packers. "In the first meeting," wrote Vince, "I gave them a camp curfew: in bed and lights out by eleven o'clock, midnight on Saturdays. Any breaking of that curfew would cost the player five hundred dollars. Any player late for a meeting or practice would be fined ten dollars a minute, and any of them caught standing at a bar would be knicked for one hundred and fifty dollars." "Wherever you go, you will represent the team," he also told them. "You will talk like, you will look like, and you will act like the most dignified professional in your hometown."

"He left no doubt what he expected," remembered Bart Starr. But, to their chagrin, Starr and the other Packer players quickly found out that their new coach could be a bit unconventional and idiosyncratic. "Lombardi time," for example, meant being fifteen minutes *early* for everything—meals, meetings, workouts, buses, curfews, everything. "I believe a man should be on time," lectured Lombardi, "not a minute late, not ten seconds late. . . . I believe that a man who's late for meetings or for the bus won't run his pass routes right."

Starr and his roommate, Gary Knafelc, were once levied a fine for arriving only seven minutes before a team bus was to depart. As far as Lombardi was concerned, they were eight minutes late—and he was waiting for them. "That'll be fifty dollars, gentlemen," he said with a stare. "It was the first time I'd ever been late for anything in my entire life," lamented Starr.

While Lombardi was strict on the enforcement of his rules, he also was evenhanded and fair. He allowed no special treatment for the "stars" on the team—as "Golden Boy" Paul Hornung learned the hard way. One night after the 11:00 curfew, Hornung and Max McGee left their room and headed downtown for a night of carousing. McGee returned at 4:30 A.M., but Hornung was still out when he received a call at 8:30 "We got caught," McGee told him. "Vince wants to see both of us together." Hornung, many years later, vividly described what happened next:

> Vince was in one of the conference rooms downstairs in the dorm, and when we walked in, he was meeting with the

coaches. He was standing at the blackboard, writing something, and as soon as he saw us, he got so worked up, the chalk broke in his hand. He started screaming so loud everybody in the dormitory could hear him. I couldn't tell exactly what he was saying at first, but I knew it wasn't complimentary. Finally, he looked at me and hollered, "Hornung! What do you want to be? A playboy or a football player?"

I don't know what got into me. "A playboy," I said.

"Get out of here!" he shouted. "Get out of here!"

He fined us five hundred and he confined us to quarters for a week. We weren't allowed to leave the dormitory except for meals and practice.

Even Vince's wife, Marie, was not exempt from the rules. At an early team dinner, she politely asked the waiter if she might have a scoop of ice cream on her apple pie. Jerry Kramer recalled that "Vince jumped out of his seat, red-faced, and bellowed: 'When you travel with the team, and you eat with the team, you eat what the team eats!'"

"I ran on Lombardi time, too," Marie said. "Vin was never late in his life."

Lombardi's blasting of his wife in front of the team, if not sensitive or smart on his part, was certainly an effective demonstration of his commitment. No one—not his team, not his family, and especially not himself—was pardoned from living by the rules. "There's nothing personal about any of this," said Lombardi. "Any fine I levy on anyone, I levy because he's hurting not only himself but thirty-five other men."

Vince also involved those other men by setting up a committee of six players to collect fines and hear appeals. As he explained it, "I took a little off it by telling them to appoint an executive committee, empowered to discuss any fines or any grievances with me, and I said that all money collected would go into a team fund. With it the team could throw a party, at a proper time, or put it to any other use that they preferred, with the restriction that none of it was to be returned to any fined player."

After Vince levied his first $500 fine, the committee protested that it was too stiff. "I told them that if we didn't set an example none of our regulations would be worth anything," remembered Lombardi, "and I told them to talk it over again." When the committee returned, they had all agreed that the fine should stand. "We were a team," recalled Emlen Tunnell, one of the committee members, "and we were determined that we'd all be winners."

Despite the stiff fines, there was not a lot of friction on the team, because after a short time almost no one broke the rules. "Actually he ended up fining fewer people less money than any coach I played for," said linebacker Dave Robinson. "He didn't have to fine them."

Lombardi was an experienced-enough leader to know that if he established his authority by *setting* the rules, *explaining* them clearly, and *enforcing* them evenhandedly, he would be successful in creating a culture of discipline on his team. "Discipline is part of the will, really," he said. "A disciplined person is one who follows the will of the one who gives the orders."

What's more, Vince knew he had a good group of guys on his team— decent men with proper values. "Truly, I have never known a really successful man who deep in his heart did not understand the grind, the discipline it takes to win," he once said. "There is something in good men that really yearns for, needs, discipline and the harsh reality of head-to-head contact."

Well, if Vince Lombardi believed his team yearned for "the harsh reality of head-to-head contact," he most certainly gave it to them in ways the players would never forget. With "ear-splitting shouts," with his nose "an inch from a player's nose," and by yelling things like, "I'm telling you for the last time, for the last goddamn time . . ." or "You are *really* something, you are, mister," Lombardi would, quite simply, *raise hell.*

"He was a force field," claimed Bill Curry. "Some people can yell at you and you chuckle because they're ridiculous the way they do it. But when he did it, it would go straight to your heart and your heart would go straight to your throat." And almost always, the players responded with better performances. Here are just a few examples:

- At one early practice, a rookie ran the same play incorrectly three times in a row. The third time, even though he had gained thirty-five yards, he found that Lombardi had chased him down the field and was right in his face screaming at him for the mistake. "Gee," the rookie said to another player, "you make a mistake and the guy throws a fit on you." But that rookie never again made the same mistake.

- When center Ken Iman missed a snap count, Lombardi yelled: "You stupid son of a bitch! How do you expect to play in this league if you can't remember the snap count?" Years later, Iman stated that "I haven't made a late snap since then."

- Displeased with the way Ray Nitschke was performing in a drill, Vince stopped everything and said: "Mr. Nitschke, I have read that you are the best linebacker in the NFL. But after watching you just then I find it hard to believe. Now, do it again!" As Paul Hornung recalled, "This time Ray grabbed the rookie by the shoulder pads, literally lifted him up, and threw him into Jimmy. It took them two minutes to get the rookie to come to."

- When Lombardi sensed that Lee Roy Caffey was loafing in practice, he pulled his linebacker aside. "Caffey, that stinks," he said. "Lee Roy, if you cheat on the practice field, you'll cheat in the game. If you cheat in the game, you'll cheat the rest of your life. I'll not have it." Caffey later became a standout linebacker in the National Football League.

Many leaders avoid confrontation, but not Vince Lombardi. As a matter of fact, Lombardi *created* confrontation. When he did so, he was getting the issue of performance out on the table. It was between him and the player he was dealing with, man to man. That guy was either going to perform or not going to perform. He had to commit to his leader to take action—or get out. When the player did so, he was also making a commitment to *himself*. In effect, then, when Lombardi confronted a member of his team, he was forcing the individual to *think* about his *personal* commitment to the organization and to his own performance. In essence, Vince Lombardi's "harsh reality of head-to-head contact," as he phrased it, was a raw, basic form of motivation that few leaders are willing to utilize. And the fact that Lombardi was able to employ it effectively—so that people, in the end, wound up *loving* him— was part of the genius of his leadership.

Lombardi knew that direct confrontation causes people to *think* seriously—to think about *what* they're doing, *why* they're doing it, and *who they are* when they're doing it. Such thinking, in turn, leads to a certain mental preparedness. And, for Lombardi, getting his players "in shape mentally" was just as important as getting them in shape physically.

"Success in anything in this world is 75 percent mental," he noted. "If you play with just your body and not your brains, you don't last long. Teams do not go physically flat, but they go mentally stale."

So Lombardi sought to develop a certain mental discipline in every member of his team. He called it mental toughness, which he defined as a combination of "singleness of purpose" (because, "success demands singleness of purpose"), "humility," and "a perfectly disciplined will." "Mental toughness is Spartanism with its qualities of sacrifice and self-denial, dedication, fearlessness, and love. [It] is a state of mind. You might call it 'character in action,'" said Lombardi. "Once you have established the goals you want and the price you're willing to pay for success, you can ignore the minor hurts, the opponent's pressure, and the temporary failures."

"Ignoring the minor hurts" was, for Vince Lombardi, an obsession— as any of his players would readily attest. "He told us that the Good Lord gave you a body that can stand most anything," remembered Ken Iman. "It's your mind you have to convince." "Hurt is in the mind," Lombardi said. "You have to play with those small hurts."

Over and over and over again, Vince *forced* his players (in a manner that some thought sadistic) to train their minds to sustain pain. For example, when Bob Long hurt his knee during practice, Lombardi yelled, "Drag him off the field and let's get on with the scrimmage!" (Long played for six weeks with torn cartilage in his knee.) When rookie guard Jerry Moore sustained a practice injury and lay writhing in pain on the ground, Lombardi ran out onto the field and screamed, "Get up! Get up off the ground! You're not hurt! You're not hurt!" During another practice, offensive end Cooper Rollow did not get up off the ground after a particularly violent collision, so the team's trainer ran on the field with an emergency medical kit. "Get away from him!" bellowed Lombardi. "Leave him alone! He either stands up on his own and becomes a Green Bay Packer or he crawls off the field and out of the league!" Lombardi also demanded that Lionel Aldridge *run*, not *jog* but *run*, just a few days after having the cast removed from his broken leg. And when guard Willie Bankstone's ankle swelled to three times its normal size, Lombardi looked at him and said, "I'll tell you this, mister: you're going to play Sunday if we have to carry you out there on a stretcher. Now run!" Bankstone ran back onto the field and also played in Sunday's game. "Coach has the highest pain threshold in the world," Jerry Kramer once quipped. "None of our injuries hurts him at all."

But Lombardi's insistence on maintaining a high threshold of pain did, in fact, translate into a tremendous disciplined will for his teams. And players, almost routinely, played with injuries that went far beyond what most people would term small hurts.

Charlie Conerly stayed in a game despite breaking his nose. Paul Hornung played with strained ligaments. Chuck Mercein played with a painful hip pointer and a shoulder separation. Elijah Pitts played *two* games with a shoulder separation. Jerry Kramer took a hit in the ribs during the first game of a road trip, shook off the pain, and played again the next week. Only when the team got back to Green Bay did the doctors tell him he had two broken ribs. Bart Starr stayed in, and won, a game despite being violently sick to his stomach. He also played an exhibition game with a shoulder separation and performed so poorly that Lombardi chastised him. "Good God! You're playing like you're crippled!" he yelled. But Starr offered no excuses and didn't say a word about his shoulder.

Like Starr, the rest of Lombardi's players rarely offered any excuses because, as Boyd Dowler said, "He hated excuses!" He demanded that they perform their jobs correctly *all* the time, that they *not* offer excuses and they *not* make mistakes—at least not *mental* mistakes. And to Vince, there was a distinct difference. "What I criticize people for is mental errors, not physical ones," he said. If a running back fumbled after a hard hit, Lombardi "would be the first one to pat him on the back and tell him to forget it." On the other hand, if a lineman jumped offside or was called for holding, Lombardi would "chew him up one side and down the other."

"By being alert you are going to make fewer mistakes than your opponents," he once told a group of rookies. "You will make mistakes—but not very many if you want to play for the Green Bay Packers."

Everybody got *that* message. "He simply wouldn't let you make mental errors," remembered Jim Ringo. "If you did, you wouldn't be with him any longer." "Nobody who played for Lombardi would ever have jumped offside and cost the club a championship," said Max McGee. "He wouldn't have permitted it."

As time progressed and Lombardi's focus on physical fitness, discipline, and mental toughness became a way of life for his football teams, winning became commonplace. And that, in turn, *thrilled* his players and *confounded* the opposition. "Lombardi conditioning is playing a full game, and not even perspiring in the fourth quarter," marveled Henry

Jordan, "when the other guys are huffing and puffing, and their eyes are getting glassy." "You always know what those goddamn Packers are going to do," complained one opposing coach, "but you can't stop them—they never make mistakes."

Even though, at the time, Lombardi's players did not enjoy or appreciate the tough regime he put them through, they gradually began to realize its long-term value. "I remember the first year he said, 'Fatigue makes cowards of us all,'" remarked Bob Skoronski. "There were a lot of guys around that day and some of them laughed and giggled. But you know, four or five years later those same guys who giggled, I heard them say to some young players, 'Hey, you had better get moving or fatigue will make cowards of you!'"

Bill Curry was equally observant in his reflections on how Lombardi had impacted him personally. "I realized he had pushed me through a sort of barrier, a self-pity barrier," he said. "He taught me that I could do things with pain, transcend it." "He made us proud of our injuries," said Sonny Jurgensen. "Coach Lombardi showed me that, by working hard and using my mind, I could overcome my weaknesses to the point where I could be one of the best," remarked an appreciative Bart Starr years later. "I learned so many things from him that will help me the rest of my life."

Perhaps while he was driving and pushing and berating and shaming his men into confronting their weaknesses, Lombardi thought about how it would make them better people in the future. "There are occasions when being hard and tough is the easiest way and the kindest way in the long run," he once said. "We have to be hard sometimes to get the most out of our people, out of ourselves."

Maybe that's why he was always in their faces—forcing each individual to confront a weakness and then driving him to overcome it. Maybe that's why he was so hard on Lionel Aldridge, for instance, when the star Packer defensive end one year showed up on the first day of one training camp overweight and out of shape. Lombardi noticed immediately and singled Lionel out as an example to the rest of the squad. He yelled, screamed, and berated Aldridge. He worked him so mercilessly in the grass drill that a concerned Ray Nitschke urged Lionel to "fall down and stay down" for his own good. But he refused to quit.

Finally, exhausted and unable to stand any more, Lionel Aldridge passed out. And when he came to, the first thing he saw was the face of his stern coach hovering over him. "Aldridge," roared Lombardi, "that's all that beer you drank in the off-season!"

Lombardi Principles

- Year-in and year-out, insist that everyone, veterans and rookies alike, prove themselves worthy of your organization.
- Good physical conditioning is essential to any occupation. A man who is physically fit performs better at any job.
- The harder you work, the harder it is to surrender.
- Winning is gained through discipline. Success demands singleness of purpose.
- Immediately set, and clearly explain, the ground rules covering behavior and conduct.
- Strictly enforce the rules, but be evenhanded and fair. Set up an employee committee to collect fines and hear appeals.
- Believe in being on time.
- You discipline yourself by refusing to give in to yourself. Once a person learns to quit, it becomes a habit.
- Do not be afraid of confrontation. Create it.
- Head-to-head confrontation forces an individual to think seriously about his personal commitment to the organization and to his own performance.
- Success in anything in this world is 75 percent mental. Teams do not go physically flat; they go mentally stale.
- Strive to develop a mental toughness in every member of your team.
- Ignore the minor hurts. Hurt is in the mind.
- Accept physical mistakes. Do not tolerate mental mistakes.
- *Offer* no excuses. *Accept* no excuses.
- You have to be hard sometimes to get the most out of your people and out of yourself.

We no longer teach our backs to run solely to that hole. We school them to run to the daylight, wherever it is.

VINCE LOMBARDI

"How's he playing you? What do you think?"
"Gee, Coach. I think I can beat him on turn-ins."
"All right, give it a try."

LOMBARDI IN CONVERSATION WITH
WIDE RECEIVER BOYD DOWLER
DURING A GAME

Don't ask any question you can answer yourself. You *take the initiative.*

VINCE LOMBARDI,
TO HIS ASSISTANT COACHES

14   *Run to Daylight*

Frank Gifford takes a handoff from the quarterback. He starts inside, just as the play calls for, but finds that the defensive end has overpowered the offensive guard and plugged up the hole he was supposed to run through. Instinctively Gifford cuts outside and sprints into the clearing for a long gainer.

Vince Lombardi is watching from the sidelines. His first reaction is negative—Gifford didn't run the play as designed. But then Lombardi realizes that if Gifford had done so, he would have gone nowhere, maybe even have lost yardage. *Damn!* thinks Lombardi. *Gifford did the right thing. Gotta do something about that play.*

This episode occurred in New York Giants training camp in 1954—and Vince would recall years later that it was "the first time I realized that, in pro football, it was to your advantage to run to daylight and not to run to a specific hole." So he immediately started coaching that particular "belly play" differently. "We no longer teach our backs to run solely to that hole," he announced to the team. "We school them to run to daylight, wherever it is." The play was changed so that if the defensive end cut the running back off, he would go to the outside, just as Gifford had done. But if the end went to the outside (as the play was originally designed), then the running back would merely follow the block of the guard and go inside. Either way, there was now a higher probability that this particular play would be a ground gainer.

This concept worked so well that by the time Vince got to the Packers, he had expanded the idea to include the offensive linemen. "Our whole running game is built around Coach Lombardi's theory of running to daylight," explained guard Jerry Kramer. "Except on special plays, you don't have any predetermined place to take the man you're blocking. You just take him where he wants to go. If he wants to go inside, I'll drive him inside and the back runs outside. If he wants to go outside, I'll drive him outside and the back runs inside." "It was just sound, simple football," recalled Vince Promuto, who learned Lombardi's theory with the Washington Redskins. "If you did it his way, there were three or four possible holes to run to. It made a lot more sense."

Even though Lombardi's concept of running to daylight offered a variety of opportunities, it was also fraught with risk because, in order to make things work effectively, smart and talented people were required to carry out the tasks. It also demanded skilled teamwork. The running backs and the offensive linemen had to work closely together to make the running game successful. Of course, everything hinged around the instinctive ability of the man with the ball. That person had to be able to take action immediately, on his own, without hesitation and certainly without asking for permission.

Vince had taken care of the people risk as soon as he arrived at Green Bay. He realized early on, from carefully watching game films, that Paul Hornung and Jim Taylor were as talented as they come. So he centered the Packer offensive attack around them (just as, years earlier, he had centered the New York Giant offensive attack around Frank Gifford). And once Vince had completed building a front line that included such intelligent and versatile guards as Fuzzy Thurston and Jerry Kramer, he had the core group of people who could make his idea work because they could both *think independently* and *work together* effectively.

However, in order for his running-to-daylight theory to work smoothly, there was one more risk Vince had to confront. He had to let go of some power. And despite his reputation for authoritarianism, empowerment and delegation were primary elements of Lombardi's leadership philosophy. "He would tell you what he wanted accomplished," remembered Henry Jordan, "and then he'd let you do it any way you wanted as long as you got the job done."

Essentially, Lombardi ran the Packers like any chief executive would run a successful business. Not only did he delegate authority to his generals; he demanded excellent performances from them. Assistant coaches were given responsibility, left alone to do their jobs, and constantly reminded to take charge. "Don't ask any question you can answer yourself," he lectured. "*You* take the initiative!" And it was the same for the players. Quarterbacks, for instance, called all the plays on the field and had the authority to change the play at the line of scrimmage with "automatics." So with the patience and skill of a Bart Starr or a Sonny Jurgensen, Vince had that "extension of himself" that he was always seeking. "He liked to establish responsibility on the field," said Willie Davis. "If you did your job," remembered end Bob Schnelker, "he really left you alone."

However, if either a coach, a player, or a member of the staff *did not* do his job well, Lombardi, *without fail*, would hold him accountable. "I don't know anything about photography," he once barked to the Packer staff film director. "But *you* damn well better know photography." And Vince, of course, was all over the players if they committed mental errors that kept them from attaining their very highest level of performance. "The cardinal sin," said Willie Davis quite simply, "was to be out-thought."

In effect, then, Vince Lombardi skillfully combined the softer leadership principles of *delegation and empowerment* with the more authoritarian concepts of *accountability and responsibility*. By doing so, he was able to elicit personal commitment from individuals. And he intuitively realized that once people are given the opportunity to succeed or fail on their own merits, they will more easily, and perhaps more naturally, accept responsibility for the outcome—whether it be positive or negative.

In addition, Lombardi was often able to come up with better ways of doing things by tapping into the minds of his players. He asked their opinions, solicited their feedback, listened carefully when they spoke, and, most important, *acted* on ideas that made sense to him—even if they were contrary to his original intentions.

"What do you think?" Vince would ask one of his assistant coaches. After a response was made, he might then say, "Gee, I didn't think of that," or, "That's a better idea." Pat Peppler pointed out that Lombardi "wasn't too big to change his mind." And Jack Stroud said that "if you proved you were right, he'd change."

But Lombardi's methods were about more than simply looking for a better idea or a better way of doing things. He also strategically sought to *involve* the players as full, bona fide partners in the organization.

"How's he playing you?" Lombardi once asked wide receiver Boyd Dowler during a game.

"Gee, Coach. I think I can beat him on turn-ins."

"All right, give it a try," Lombardi responded.

Henry Jordan, reflecting on his coach's methods many years later, observed that "this little technique of his worked two ways. First, he got the opinion of a veteran, and second, he made [us] feel a part of everything. He did this with all the guys. He knew what he was doing; he was a very intelligent man."

"Running to daylight" revolved around making decisions on the run. The players not only had to have "poise and confidence," as Vince said, but they also had "to make the quick decision necessary if the running-to-daylight option is to work."

All Green Bay offensive plays were designed to work against a particular defense. However, if the opposing team changed its defensive setup during the game (which frequently occurred), Lombardi wanted his players to be able to adjust *their* tactics and patterns to fit whatever the defense was throwing at them. So he designed plays with a variety of options that allowed his players to react instantly to possible defensive variations.

A good example of this successful "adjustment on the fly" occurred in the Packers' 1961 championship victory over New York when the Giants undershifted their defensive line in order to stop Jim Taylor. "We countered by running the ball right at the middle linebacker, who was playing over the guard," explained Lombardi. "This gave Taylor three potential holes to hit. If the middle linebacker came to the right, he went to the left; if the middle linebacker went to the left, he went to the right; and if the defensive end closed down hard to the inside, then Taylor just went outside of that defensive end's force and the offensive tackle let the defensive end come to the inside. Taylor got a great deal of daylight to run to. And on one particular play, Jimmy broke it for about a 45-yard run."

Essentially, that's the way things worked on Lombardi teams—routinely adjusting on the fly, habitually creating new options, instinctively running to daylight wherever it was. "He expected people to think on the field to the degree that it could come automatically," said center Jim Ringo. "His teams always adjusted easily," noted Pat Peppler. "It got to be like brushing their teeth and combing their hair."

All told, Vince Lombardi set up his Packer team to run like an efficient, nimble-footed, start-up business—as opposed to a bureaucratic, "always-first-check-with-the-boss," slow-moving megaconglomerate. In other words, he wanted his organization to operate more like an entrepreneur than a large corporation. And he especially wanted his players to take risks and act on their own initiative while on the playing field—particularly when the opposition gave them an opening.

Whenever the offense observed defensive linebackers lining up inside, for instance, the quarterback was encouraged to call an "automatic" pass play—and the receivers were schooled to expect it. In that situation, Lombardi "demanded that you throw the ball," remembered quarterback Zeke Bratkowski. "Just throw the ball because your percentage was going to be high. He expected it to be high. He demanded it to be high. I mean, he would be very loud—'THROW THE BALL!'"

And Lombardi did not seem to worry about the danger of a potential interception in such a circumstance. "I don't like to use the term *gambler's instinct*," he said, "but I'm willing to take a chance."

Overall, Vince Lombardi's concept of running to daylight involved much more than simply heading toward an open space. It also included taking risks, taking initiative, creating and exercising options, adjusting on the fly, and making on-the-spot decisions. However, there was one more very important principle, which was perceptively noticed by Redskin running back Larry Brown. "He meant a little more than most people realized by this thing he called running to daylight," explained Brown. "He meant doing it in one continuous motion. If the hole is plugged you don't stop to look for another one. You keep running—keep accelerating—as you look."

Lombardi himself called this principle " 'second effort'—that tenacity to give it one more try." If any one of his players saw a chance to run to daylight, he was to take it. "Football is a game of abandon," Lombardi would say to his running backs. "You care nothing for anybody or anything, and when you get close to the goal line, your abandon is intensified. Nothing, not a tank, not a wall, not a dozen men, can stop you from getting across that goal line. If I ever see one of my backs get stopped a yard from the goal line, I'll come off that bench and kick him right in the can!"

At the end of the day, Vince Lombardi realized that once the players were in a game and on the playing field, there wasn't very much that he, as their coach and leader, could do to affect the outcome.

And, not surprisingly, the football players on his team realized it, too. In fact, the Green Bay Packers had a running joke about it. "We have the greatest coach in the world," it went, "but once the game gets started, Lombardi is the most useless guy on the sidelines."

Lombardi Principles

- School your people to run to daylight, wherever it is.
- Increase the probability that any play you run will be a ground gainer.
- Encourage people to take action immediately, on their own, and without asking for permission.
- Tell your people what needs to be accomplished and let them do it any way they want as long as the job gets done.
- Delegate authority, demand excellent performance, and hold people accountable.
- Don't ask any question you can answer yourself. Take the initiative.
- Remember that the cardinal sin is to be out-thought.
- Combine the softer leadership principles of delegation and empowerment with the more authoritarian concepts of accountability and responsibility.
- Ask people what they think. You'll not only get the opinions of experienced veterans; you'll also make people feel a part of everything.
- Design options that will allow people to react instantly to changing conditions.
- Teach people to think on the field to the degree that it comes automatically.
- Operate your organization more like an entrepreneur than a large corporation.
- Be willing to take a chance. THROW THE BALL.
- Don't stop to look. Keep running—keep accelerating—*as you look*.
- Make that "second effort"—have the tenacity to give it one more try.

The purpose of the game is to win. To dilute the will to win is to destroy the purpose of the game.

RED BLAIK,
VINCE LOMBARDI'S MENTOR

The strength of the group is in the will of the leader, and the will is character in action.

VINCE LOMBARDI

Winning isn't everything; it's the only thing.

VINCE LOMBARDI

15   Have the Will to Win

"GODDAMMIT, YOU GUYS DON'T CARE IF YOU WIN OR LOSE! I'M THE ONLY ONE WHO CARES! I'm the only one who puts his blood and his guts and his heart into the game! You guys show up; you listen a little bit! You've got the concentration of three-year-olds! YOU'RE NOTHING! I'M THE ONLY GUY WHO GIVES A DAMN IF WE WIN OR LOSE!"

These were the irate words of Vince Lombardi on Tuesday, November 30, 1965. Two days earlier, in their eleventh game of the season, the Packers had lost to the last-place Los Angeles Rams, 21–10, lowering their record to 8–3. Upon arriving at work that morning, Lombardi ordered his assistant coaches out of the team locker room. Then he began his assault on the players by questioning the "ancestry" of Lionel Aldridge, who had made the mistake of singing a happy tune on the plane ride back to Green Bay. Next Vince launched into a screaming fury that Bill Curry later described as nothing less than "one of those tirades you'd see in films of Hitler going through a frenzy."

"I DON'T THINK ANYBODY IN THIS ROOM WANTS TO PLAY FOOTBALL!" he yelled. "I can't think of a soul in here who wants to play! In fact, I don't think any of you will stand up and tell me that you do! No one in this room wants to pay the price! I'M THE ONLY ONE HERE WHO'S WILLING TO PAY THE PRICE! YOU GUYS DON'T CARE! YOU DON'T WANT TO WIN!"

Finally, Forrest Gregg could stand no more. Red with rage and bursting with fury, he stood up and lunged toward his coach. Fortunately, teammates on both sides grabbed his arms and held him back. "Goddammit, Coach!" yelled Gregg. "'Scuse the language, Coach, but goddammit, it makes me sick to hear you say something like that. I want to win. It tears my guts out to lose. We lay our ass on the line for you every Sunday. We live and die the same way you do, and it hurts."

Then Bob Skoronski bolted upright. "That's right! Don't tell us that we don't care about winning!" he hollered at Lombardi. "That makes me sick! Makes me want to puke! We care about it every bit as much as you do! It's *our* knees and *our* bodies that we're throwing around!"

"All right!" said Lombardi in an approving tone. "Now that's the kind of attitude I want to see. Who else feels that way?"

Just then, Willie Davis, who had been leaning his chair on two legs, lost his balance and fell forward into the middle of the room. Embarrassed, he picked himself up off the floor and sheepishly said, "Yeah, me, too, Coach. I feel that way, man. I want to win."

Lombardi immediately burst out laughing, which may have served as a cue to the rest of the guys. Because the next thing he knew, all forty players were on their feet shouting, "I want to win!" "Me, too, Coach, I want to win!" "Yeah, I want to win!"

Bart Starr, who was one of the first on his feet after Davis, felt that Lombardi *wanted* the players to stand and defy him. "We were practically in tears because he had challenged our very being. I think he had a definite purpose in doing so. He could see we were about to be deeply involved in some sort of slump, and I think maybe this was his way of jacking us out of it." Willie Davis concurred by noting that Coach Lombardi "never let us slip into a defeatist attitude. Never."

The Green Bay Packers did not lose another game that season. They played three more in the regular season, two in the play-offs, and brought home the NFL championship.

If the Packer players were surprised at their coach's intensity that day, they shouldn't have been. Rather, they should have been getting used to it because, from day one of his tenure in Green Bay, Lombardi had told them what to expect. "I will put winning above all else here," he said in 1960. And he reinforced that tenet regularly over the decade he led the Packers.

"I'm going to tell you the facts, gentlemen, and the facts are these!" he bellowed on a Tuesday morning in 1967. "At Green Bay, we have winners. We do not have losers. If you're a loser, mister, you're going to get your ass out of here and you're going to get your ass out of here right now! Gentlemen, we are paid to win! Gentlemen, we *will* win." After that particular speech, a stunned Lee Roy Caffey turned to Jerry Kramer and asked, "Who the hell won that game, anyhow?" Caffey was shocked because Lombardi's speech had come after the Packers had *beaten* the Dallas Cowboys, 20–3, with a sloppy performance in a *preseason* game.

There's no question that part of Vince Lombardi's definition of success in his profession was winning football games. That philosophy had been drilled into him when he was at West Point. "The purpose of the game is to win," Red Blaik often said. "To dilute the will to win is to destroy the purpose of the game." And General Douglas MacArthur, one of Lombardi's heroes, with whom he sometimes spoke personally, had said: "There is no substitute for victory."

So by the time Vince became a head coach in professional football, winning was not only a habitual part of his character; it was a mandatory corporate mission, because it was the only thing that would ensure the survival of his organization. "We're in the *business* of winning ball games," Lombardi noted. "That scoreboard controls your economic future and your prestige. The best way to keep the stadium filled is with a championship team."

Therefore, Lombardi wanted nothing whatsoever to do with finishing in second place, which he termed as "meaningless" and "hinky-dinky." "In our business, there *is* no second place," he said. "Either you're first or you're last."

It was because of this "no-second-place" mandate that Vince constantly lectured his players that "there is no substitute for winning," that every player had to "be a hard loser," that they had to try their "damnedest to win every game no matter what," that they should "never be ready to settle for a tie," and that "if you could have won, you should have won."

Furthermore, Lombardi believed success on the football field would have a strategic motivational impact on his team in three important ways:

First, once the team started winning on a regular basis, success would become a matter of routine. "Winning is like a drug," said Lombardi. "It's a hard thing to kick. It saps your elation in victory and deepens your despair in defeat. [But] once you have sampled it, you are hooked. Winning is a habit. Unfortunately, so is losing."

Second, success transforms the mood of an organization to spirited and fun-loving. "We were the happiest group of people," remembered Packer public relations director Tom Miller. "Winning made it that way. I was here when we were losers, before Lombardi and after; and believe me, you're a lot happier when you're a winner." Vince knew that winning was fun for everybody involved—and people who are having fun at their jobs will perform much better. "Football is a game that gives one hundred percent fun when you win," he said, "and exacts a one hundred percent resolution when you lose."

Third, success instills confidence in a team, which, in turn, serves to perpetuate even more success. "You'd be surprised how much confidence a little success will bring," Vince noted. "Confidence is contagious." To a man, his players agreed. "I *knew* we were going to win every game we played," said Willie Davis. "And the more important it was for us to win, the more certain I was we would win." "There was never any doubt," recalled running back Chuck Mercein. "There just was never any doubt on the field, in the huddle, or on the sideline."

Essentially, then, winning was not only Lombardi's definition of success in football; it also served as a primary form of motivation. But everyone who knew Vince realized that there was more to it than that— much more. Winning for him was part of an innate drive to achieve—an incredibly persistent desire to attain success.

To Willie Davis, "[Lombardi] was driven." To Bill Heinz, he had "an almost fanatical desire" to win. "He was probably the most totally competitive—around-the-clock, through the calendar—man I have ever met," said Heinz. "I've never met anyone that competitive," said Tom Landry. Others described Lombardi as "a man in a hurry," a person who was "incapable of relaxing too long," and a guy who "would never, ever give up."

Lombardi himself readily admitted this innate intensity to achieve, often describing it as "that fire in you" and "the flame that burns inside." "There's more to life than just being contented," he said. "I *thrive* on work. . . . I have *got* to win. . . . I know of no way but to persist."

Moreover, Vince had always been that way—even when he was a kid growing up in Brooklyn. "I had this drive to be the best in everything," he explained to a journalist. "I wasn't born with much size or speed, and so everything I did in the field of athletics was a struggle. I had to try harder than anyone else. But there is something to be said for that kind of an attitude, because I found that if I really wanted something badly enough, it was possible. I always tried to want it more than the other kids. That was my edge."

And when he became a head football coach, Lombardi's edge became the Green Bay Packers' edge—because he would do nearly anything it took to win ball games. A good example occurred during the heat of the 1961 Berlin Crisis. That fall, President John F. Kennedy had ordered a troop buildup in Germany, which resulted in a call-up of reserves. When Paul Hornung, Ray Nitschke, and Boyd Dowler were summoned, Lombardi sprang into action. He did not hesitate to call on old friends from his days at West Point. And through one of them, he received access to President Kennedy's military adviser and was able to adjust the schedules of all three players so they could play ball on Sundays. Then, when the Packers made it all the way to the championship game, Dowler and Nitschke received special passes, but superstar Paul Horning's pass was overlooked. When Vince found out, he picked up the phone and called the White House. In less than a minute he was speaking to President Kennedy and explaining the problem. "Coach," replied Kennedy, "Paul Hornung isn't going to win the war on Sunday, but the football fans of this country deserve the two best teams on the field that day." Horning not only made it to the game; he also rushed for one touchdown and kicked three field goals and four points after touchdown, thereby setting an NFL record of nineteen points. The Packers won that game 37–0 over the New York Giants for their first NFL championship—in part because their coach would not let the United States Armed Forces rob him of three star players.

Five years later, on December 18, 1966, the Packers played their last game of the regular season against the Rams in Los Angeles. It would have been an easy game for the team to sit back and relax a bit, because they had clinched the Western Conference title the week before. But, as linebacker Bill Forrester noted of his coach, "You couldn't believe how much he wanted to win the games that didn't count—after we had clinched our division title."

All week in practice Lombardi angrily drove his team because they were seemingly uninspired. They had "a lackadaisical attitude," he told them.

Have the Will to Win

They didn't "have any pride," he told them. All they had was "shame," he said. They were "a disgrace to the National Football League," he said. In the locker room before the game, Vince told the players that if they didn't give their best effort they would be cheating themselves, everybody in Green Bay, and "the Maker who gave you that talent." "I know we don't have cheaters on this ball club," were his final words before the team took the field. After the Packers defeated the Rams, 27–23, reporters wondered why they had played with such intensity. A proud Vince Lombardi responded: "Anytime you've got a God-given talent," he said, "you should use it at all times, and that's the way it turned out today."

Reflecting on that entire week, Bart Starr commented: "Sometimes I think no game we ever played for Coach Lombardi gave him as much satisfaction as the one we didn't have to win but did." (Green Bay went on to win the first Super Bowl that year.)

The next year, 1967, the Packers found themselves playing Los Angeles in the first game of the play-offs. With a record of 11-1-2, the Rams were heavily favored to knock off the aging and injured defending champions. As a matter of fact, they had already beaten the Packers just the previous week. But, as far as Lombardi was concerned, this time the outcome would be different. On the Tuesday before the game, Lombardi gave his team an impassioned speech. "We may be wounded," he said. "We may be in trouble. But I'll tell you one thing: That damned Los Angeles better be ready to play a football game when they come in here, 'cause they're going to have a battle. I'll guarantee that. This team has a history of rising to the occasion. THIS IS IT! THERE'S NO TOMOR-ROW! THIS REALLY IS THE START OF THE BIG PUSH!"

Then Lombardi pulled out his Bible and read to the team St. Paul's First Epistle to the Corinthians, ninth chapter, twenty-fourth verse:

"Brethren: Don't you know that while all the runners in the stadium take part in the race, only one wins the prize. Run to win."

Many players recalled later that this speech, in particular, really impacted them. Ray Nitschke remembered that "I kept saying to myself, 'I'm running to win. I'm running to win.'" Others felt the same way, because on that day the Packers defeated Los Angeles by a lopsided score of 28–7. Then they went on to win Super Bowl II.

During his entire career, Vince Lombardi, quite literally, refused to lose ball games. In what many people call one of the greatest championship games in NFL history—where the Baltimore Colts defeated the New York Giants in overtime to win the 1958 NFL championship—

Vince was on the Giants sideline as an assistant coach along with Tom Landry. But where Landry accepted the loss and reflected that "it marked the time, the game, and the place where pro football really caught on," Lombardi refused to admit that the Giants had lost the game. "I have *never* lost a football game!" he declared. "Never! Now, a few times the clock runs out too early. But that doesn't mean we would've lost, because if we'd had one more minute or one more quarter—if we'd played long enough—we would've caught 'em and beat 'em."

This refusal to lose, to even admit that he had lost a game, was a matter of conscious resolve on Lombardi's part. If he *refused* to lose, he reasoned, then he would *not* lose. It was nothing less than a matter of will. And "will" was a primary component in Vince Lombardi's leadership philosophy. "The obvious difference between the group and the man who leads them is not in lack of strength, nor in lack of knowledge, but in lack of will," he said. "The strength of the group is in the will of the leader, and the will is character in action."

With this line of thinking, then, it's understandable why Lombardi frequently spoke admiringly of leaders and "the will to win." He encouraged his audiences to "cheer for, to stand up for, to stand behind the doer, the achiever, the one who recognizes a problem and does something about it . . . , the winner, the leader." To one group of businessmen, he said: "All of the display, all of the noise, all of the glamour, and all of the color and excitement, they exist only in the memory. But the spirit, the will to excel, the will to win, they endure; they last forever. These are the qualities, I think, that are larger and more important than any of the events that occasion them."

In the end, Vince believed that he, like all leaders, would "be judged by only one thing—the result." Therefore, he constantly preached that "success is not a sometime thing; it's an all-the-time thing" and that "winning isn't everything; it's the only thing." "You all know what my coaching creed is," he told the Washington Redskins in 1970, "and that is to win and to win and to win."

It was this philosophy that Vince drilled into his players. "He taught us that you must have a flaming desire to win," said Bart Starr. "It's got to dominate all your waking hours." Linebacker Dan Currie agreed: "Before Lombardi, it was sort of understood we'd try to do our best, but we'd likely lose. The main thing was to come close. *Not with Vince*," concluded Currie. "We were trained to *win*."

Lombardi himself defined happiness as "the achievement of one's objective." And what was his objective? That was simple, according to famed sportswriter Red Smith. It was "merely to win every preseason exhibition, every game during the season, every postseason game, and every title. Give him that, and he'll ask for nothing else." And Vince admitted as much after he read Smith's comment. "We never won as many as I wanted," he said, "which was all of them."

Winning dominated Lombardi's every waking moment. It consumed him. Achievement was part of who he was and, in a way, was his reason for living. "I firmly believe that any man's finest hour, his greatest fulfillment to all he holds dear," said Lombardi, "is that moment when he has worked his heart out in a good cause and lies exhausted on the field of battle—victorious!"

| | |

The night before Green Bay played New York in the 1962 NFL championship game, Vince had dinner with his mentor, former West Point head coach Red Blaik. The two talked about the big game, about football in general, and about old times. Suddenly, without warning and for no apparent reason, Vince stood up and shouted, "WE'RE GOING TO WIN!" Then, recalled Blaik, Vince "bolted out, not saying good night or good-bye or anything."

The next day, the Packers defeated the Giants, 16–7, for a second straight NFL championship.

Lombardi Principles

- Never let your team slip into a defeatist attitude. Never.
- Remember that there is no second place. Second place is meaningless and hinky-dinky.
- Never be ready to settle for a tie.
- If you could have won, you should have won.
- Remember that winning is a habit. Unfortunately, so is losing.
- Winning provides motivational impact for your team. Once you establish success, it becomes a matter of routine; it makes the job fun, and it instills a contagious confidence.
- You must want to win the games you don't have to win— because anytime you've got a God-given talent, you should use it at all times.
- No leader, however great, can long endure unless he wins battles.
- Remember, the strength of the group is in the will of the leader.
- The spirit, the will to excel, the will to win, they endure; they last forever. These qualities are larger and more important than any events that occasion them.
- Refuse to lose.
- Run to win.

Green Bay finished the 1966 regular season with a 12–2 record and defeated the Dallas Cowboys 34–27 in the NFL championship game. But they had to play one more game—Commissioner Pete Rozelle's brainchild "Super Bowl," which pitted the best team in the National Football League against the best team in the upstart American Football League. The fledging American Football League had recruited players from the National Football League and driven player salaries up. The AFL teams were considered inferior by the old guard of the National Football League—and many team owners wanted to bury the new league once and for all. So there was tremendous pressure on the Packers to win, and win decisively. The pressure was felt by Vince Lombardi. "It wasn't only Packer prestige," he later said, "but the whole NFL [that] was on the line. We had everything to lose and nothing to gain."

Their opponent was to be the Kansas City Chiefs, a strong team led by star quarterback Len Dawson and coached by the cagey Hank Stram. The Chiefs had finished the regular season with an impressive 11-2-1 record and then had blown away Buffalo in the AFL championship game. Leading up to the Super Bowl, Lombardi had been doubly hard on his team. He imposed tight curfews. Practices were serious, businesslike, and unbelievably intense. "He like to have killed us," recalled Bob Skoronski. Vince also touted the strength and ability of the Kansas City Chiefs as a formidable opponent. "He scared us to death," remembered Forrest Gregg.

The first Super Bowl was played in Los Angeles on January 15, 1967. Sixty-two thousand people were in the stands, and another 65 million viewers were tuned in to national television coverage by both CBS and NBC. Green Bay was favored by almost two touchdowns. On the team bus ride to the stadium, Lombardi stood up in the aisle and began to dance a soft-shoe. "Go, Coach, go!" yelled the players in approval. "What was that all about?" asked an assistant coach afterward. "They were too tight," replied Lombardi.

The Packers scored first on a thirty-seven-yard touchdown pass from Bart Starr to Max McGee (who had no sleep the night before because he had broken curfew and gone carousing). But the Chiefs fought back in the second period as Len Dawson engineered a long drive that culminated in a short touchdown pass to running back Curtis McClinton. It was a surprisingly close game at halftime, with the Packers clinging to a 14–10 lead.

In the locker room, Lombardi told his team that they were too nervous. "Now, I want you to go out there and make Kansas City adjust to you," he demanded. Then he ordered the defense to charge the quarterback with a series of all-out linebacker blitzes. The Packers came out on fire for the second half. A fierce pass rush quickly forced an errant pass from Dawson, which was intercepted and returned to the Chief five-yard line by Green Bay defensive back Willie Wood. Elijah Pitts scored a touchdown on the next play, and Kansas City never recovered. At the end of the day, the Green Bay Packers had won Super Bowl I by a lopsided score of 35–10.

After the game, Lombardi complimented the Kansas City Chiefs and tried to avoid any comparison of the National Football League to the American Football League. But pressed by a relentless cadre of reporters, he finally said, "That's a good football team, but it is not as good as the top teams in our league." Vince always regretted making that statement. "I came off as an ungracious winner," he told a friend. "It was lousy."

PART IV
Character

The great hope of society is the individual character. If we would create something, we must be something.

VINCE LOMBARDI

What is defeat? Nothing but education, nothing but the first step to something better. It is defeat that turns the bones to flint and gristle to muscle and makes men invincible. Do not be afraid of defeat.

VINCE LOMBARDI

The greatest glory is being knocked to your knees and then rising again.

VINCE LOMBARDI

There's no way you can hoodwink the players.

VINCE LOMBARDI

16   Have the Courage to Lead

After the Green Bay Packers had won back-to-back NFL championships in 1961 and 1962, they missed the play-offs two years running—despite compiling winning records of 11-2-1 and 8-5-1, respectively. The Chicago Bears won the 1963 championship game, 14–10, over New York in 1963, and the Cleveland Browns trounced Baltimore 27–0 in 1964. But during the 1965 season, the Packers returned with a vengeance. After finishing the regular season 10-3-1, they defeated the Colts, 13–10, in a Western Conference play-off game and then went on to beat the defending champion Browns, 23–12, to recapture the NFL title. The Pack was back—and so was Vince Lombardi.

Following the big victory, there was praise and acclaim for Lombardi's "best coaching job" to date. However, after a few days, and for the first time in his career, Vince was severely criticized for the way he led his teams to victory. Articles by the Associated Press, *New York Post*, and *New York Times* stated that Lombardi had "bullied," "harassed," and "ragged" the Packers while coercing them with everything he could think of short of "thumbscrews." He had decorated his office in "dictator modern," they wrote. His stare was "sterner than Green Bay's weather," they said. "An entire American city basks in his infrequent, crooked-tooth smiles, and his wife tolerates being tuned out at least six months a year," they charged.

Over the next several seasons, as the Packers kept winning, Vince not only received more acclaim; he was also subjected to heightened criticism. Stories in *Time* labeled him "a chubby pip-squeak with glasses" and "a sadistic dictator." Others in *Newsweek* called him "cold," "tyrannical," and "vicious" and suggested that he used "psychic manipulation" to induce his players to perform. Some critics labeled him "ruthless" and "cruel." Lombardi, they said, "was not Albert Schweitzer" but more like "Simon Legree" or "Mussolini." Moreover, as time passed, the attacks became increasingly personal in nature. Lombardi looked like "an angry jungle animal," who was "overweight," "frigidly aloof," even "fiendish." He was "interested only in his own image," "impolite even to his wife"—and had "yellow teeth with wide spaces" to boot.

At first, Vince was stunned by all the criticism. "Why would people say these terrible things about me?" he wondered. But after the initial shock wore off, he found himself deeply hurt. And even though he attempted to make jokes or laugh off the attacks, he became genuinely distraught and depressed.

For guidance and sustenance, Vince turned to close friends and colleagues. Perhaps the best piece of advice he received came from Paul Brown, head coach of the Cleveland Browns. "I just think you ought to live with it and be yourself," Paul told him. "The truth will eventually come out as to the kind of person you really are."

With solid support like that, from people who believed in him, Vince's hurt feelings gradually faded and were replaced with anger. He grew especially upset that his wife had been mentioned in the attacks. Any animosity, however, was relatively short-lived. Rather, Vince began to think deeply about *what* had happened, *why* it had happened, and *how* he should handle such criticism in the future. Eventually, he realized that the nature of his success as a leader, coupled with the nationwide media coverage the Packers were attaining, made it inevitable that he would be attacked in some way. "Once you're on top, everybody wants to knock you off," he noted. Essentially, Lombardi realized that personal slander was a fact of life—a rudiment of human nature. "I expect I will get criticized," he finally admitted to himself. And he determined that he "had to develop a thick skin to criticism and let caustic comments pass over his head."

With time, Lombardi handled the criticism that comes with leadership much the same way he dealt with losing a football game. "It takes about twelve hours for me to get over [a loss]," he observed. After that, Vince was filled with resolve and determination. His attitude became: "To hell with it! It was just a temporary loss of pride." This was precisely the same feeling he attempted to instill in the members of his team. Willie Davis once commented that, after a while, the Packers "never got shook" by losing. "We didn't ever like it," remembered Davis, "but we became more realistic about it." In part, then, Lombardi had to remind himself of the tenet he had always been preaching to his players. "If you don't put it behind you, you'll be wading around all week knee-deep in confusion," he would say. "If you can't accept losing, you can't win."

Lombardi's ability to learn from experience also aided him in dealing with thrashings—whether they were at the hands of Dallas Cowboys or the *New York Times*. "What is defeat?" Vince would ask his teams. "Nothing but education, nothing but the first step to something better. It is defeat that turns the bones to flint and gristle to muscle and makes men invincible. Do not be afraid of defeat!"

In effect, then, Lombardi viewed defeat as "an obstacle to overcome," "an opportunity to learn," or an "adversity" that provided a chance to "rise to the occasion." "Adversity is the first path to truth," he would say. "Prosperity is a great teacher; adversity is greater."

Inevitably, criticism—any criticism—also caused Lombardi to become more aware of how his behavior impacted those around him. And if he was not always more sensitive to people, he would usually take the time to explain himself and his reasoning for certain actions. However, Vince was *equally* careful not to alter his way of doing things so much that it impacted a successful outcome or, more important, so that it changed the nature of the man he was inside. "If you alter your personality just to accomplish something, you're not being true," he reasoned. "You're being dishonest."

For Lombardi, *honesty* was one of two primary elements of personal character. "A leader must be honest with himself and the people he is working with," said Vince. "He must get across to the players that feeling of truth, that feeling of honesty, that feeling of selflessness." In what is a statement remarkably similar to Abraham Lincoln's dictum "you can't fool all of the people all of the time," Lombardi also noted that "there's no way you can hoodwink the players." And he never, ever attempted to do so. He told his teams what he was all about—good and bad. He let them know where they stood—up or down. And he made sure they realized that when he promised them something, they could depend on him following through. "I don't give my word lightly," Vince told his men, "and I don't ever break it." The players recognized this uncommon honesty and responded to it. "I was able to give for him just because of what he represented in himself," noted Lionel Aldridge.

To a man, the Green Bay Packers came to recognize that the foundation of Vince Lombardi—his personality, his leadership philosophy, the way he lived his life—was an expression of his own personal character. They not only observed his character in the actions he took; they also constantly heard him speak on the subject. "Character is a man's greatest need to safeguard, because character is higher than the intellect," he would preach. "The great hope of society is the individual character," he would lecture.

Courage was the second of the two primary elements in Vince Lombardi's character—the courage to "put out that extra something," the courage to "prove what character you really have," the courage "to take it." That's the kind of courage that Lombardi admired in people. However, when it came to the members of his team, as Frank Gifford observed, "It wasn't a matter of choice. He *demanded* that courage." He encouraged his men "to move on 'guts' while they were on the playing field." "You must forget about being cautious," he told them, "because if you don't, you're licked before you start." And he especially desired that they stand up for what they believed in. "He wanted you to stand up to him, to fight back," said Sam Huff. "When he'd get mad at someone he'd go back in his office and he'd say, 'I wish that son of a bitch would stand up and say what he thinks!'" With time, Packer players learned that "the best way to get along with Lombardi was to fight right back [because] he liked that."

Vince admired courage in an individual because he believed, as Aristotle said, that "the first and most basic of the moral virtues is courage" and, as Winston Churchill said, that "courage is the greatest of all human qualities because it guarantees all the others." Without courage, people have no chance to persevere, no chance to succeed, no chance to be great.

Lombardi understood that there is a price a leader has to pay for being out in front. He knew that, at times, he was going to stumble, or fall, or make mistakes. And he realized from personal experience that others would try to drag him down, knock him down, hold him down. In essence, then, it was that same quality—the courage he tried to instill in his players—that helped *him* persevere, succeed, and become great in his own right.

"Any place I go somebody wants to fight me," Vince confided to his good friend Jim Lawlor. "I got knocked on my ass not more than two weeks ago. Tom Miller and I were coming from some place in northern Wisconsin and we stopped for a beer. It was a hot day and I'm halfway through my beer sitting on the stool and some drunk walks up and punches me right in the mouth and says, 'I just wanted to see how tough you were.'"

Vince simply picked himself up off the floor, dusted himself off, and went back to his beer. He handled that particular situation much the same way he dealt with a Packer loss to the Detroit Lions in 1962. On November 22, the Lions snapped Green Bay's impressive eighteen-game winning streak that dated back to the previous year. "This is one game—ONE GAME!" he told his dejected players in the locker room after the loss. We're going to come back. I know we are. We just have to button up our pride and we will come back. Remember, the greatest glory is being knocked to your knees and then rising again."

Lombardi Principles

- When you are victimized by unjust criticism and slander, seek the advice of close friends and colleagues.
- Once you attain a certain amount of success, it is inevitable that you'll be criticized.
- Develop a thick skin to criticism and let caustic comments pass over your head.
- If you don't put defeat behind you, you'll be wading around all week knee-deep in confusion. If you can't accept losing, you can't win.
- Defeat is nothing but education, nothing but the first step to something better.
- Adversity is the first path to truth, learn from it—but be careful not to let it change who you are inside.
- If you alter your personality just to accomplish something, you're not being true; you're being dishonest.
- Be honest with yourself and the people you are working with. Remember, there's no way you can hoodwink the players.
- Don't give your word lightly—and *never* break it.
- Forget about being cautious, because if you don't, you're licked before you start.
- There must be truth in the purpose and willpower in the character.
- The measure of a man is how he meets his failures. If he does not quit or curl up, he has the right stuff in him. The greatest accomplishment is not in never falling but in rising again after you fall.
- Do not be afraid to be a leader.

Like my father before me, I have a violent temper with which I have been struggling all my life, and with which I have had to effect a compromise. It is ineradicable, but it must not be irrational. I coach with everything that is within me, and I employ that temper for a purpose.

VINCE LOMBARDI

He was tough and abusive and at times he was downright nasty.

BART STARR,
QUARTERBACK, GREEN BAY PACKERS

I made a mistake.

ONE OF LOMBARDI'S
FREQUENT APOLOGIES

17   *Control Your Darker Side*

The Packers were in Los Angeles to play the Rams for the last game of the 1960 season. If they won, Green Bay would capture their division title. The day before the game, Lombardi, Phil Bengtson, and Norb Hecker had worked all afternoon preparing and finalizing strategy. At last, Vince suggested that they all go grab some dinner. And when Hecker recommended a place across from the hotel where the players often went to have a few beers, Lombardi agreeably replied, "Okay, let's go there."

Walking into the restaurant, the three coaches noticed some of their players sitting at a table with some drinks. Everybody waved to one another and smiled. It was okay for players to be out drinking as long as they sat at a table, according to Lombardi. "But don't ever let me catch you up at a bar!" he had admonished all of the Packers in what was regarded as one of his more stern rules.

As they headed to a booth in the back of the place, they passed a lounge on the left and saw Ray Nitschke sitting up at the bar with a beer in his hand. Caught outright, Nitschke just smiled and said, "Hi, Coach." Lombardi frowned, furled his eyebrows, and stalked to the back booth followed closely by Hecker and Bengtson. Then they sat down and began picking at a basket of peanuts on the table, breaking the shells and nibbling at the peanuts inside. After a few moments, a waiter showed up with a scotch, a bourbon, and a beer—just what the coaches usually drank.

"Who ordered these drinks?" asked Lombardi. "We didn't order any drinks. Who bought these?"

"That gentleman at the bar," said the waiter, pointing to Nitschke.

"And Jesus," remembered Norb Hecker, "Vince's hand dove into the bowl of peanuts, I'll never forget it, and he started to crunch the shells, and I could see the blood starting to flow, and he got redder and redder."

"Let's get out of here!" shouted Lombardi as he bolted away from the table toward the front entrance.

With his eyes blinking furiously and his neck turning red—"and getting redder and redder," as Hecker noted—Vince kept staring straight ahead as he walked by the bar. "YOU'RE ALL DONE!" he thundered at Nitschke. "YOU'RE THROUGH! GET OUT OF TOWN!"

Lombardi exited the establishment and walked quickly down the street with Bengtson at his heels and Hecker a distant third. Bengtson, who was the coach of the defense, began pleading with Lombardi to let Nitschke stay. "We have no other extra linebackers," said Phil. "And we've got to win Sunday. We've got to beat the Rams. We need him."

"HE'S ALL THROUGH!" screamed Lombardi. "Get him out of town! He's done! I can't stand that!"

The men finally spotted another restaurant and ducked inside. And all through their meal, Bengtson kept begging Vince to change his mind. "What are we going to do?" he asked. "What are we going to do?"

"I don't care!" snapped a still-angry Lombardi. "Get rid of him. I don't want him around here."

After some time had passed, though, and he had finished his meal, Vince began to *cool* down, but he would not *back* down. When Bengtson asked one more time to let Nitschke stay, Vince at last said: "Tell you what—we'll leave it up to the players to decide." The next morning, the Packers voted 39–0 to keep Ray Nitschke on the team.

The defining moment in this story is the instant Vince Lombardi's hand dove into that bowl of peanuts. In a split second, without warning, he had completely lost control of his emotions. And in order to vitiate his temper, Vince had to physically take it out on something. So he pulverized a bowl of peanut shells—which happened to be the nearest thing to him.

This kind of behavior was nothing new for people who were close to Lombardi. They knew that emotions ran deep within the man, that he was volatile and aggressive, that he wore his heart on his sleeve, that he sometimes took things too seriously and, all too often, he let little things bother him. Without question, these tendencies were innate—and something Lombardi could not prevent. His eyes blinked uncontrollably when he became angry. His stomach became upset. When he was frustrated, worried, or distressed, he would drive his wife crazy by cleaning out all the closets in the house. "He would take everything out of the closet and pile it in the middle of the room," said Marie Lombardi, "and then he'd look at me and say, 'What in hell do I do now?'" And according to his son, Vince Jr., "there were a few times on the sidelines when he'd get so mad that he'd literally pass out and need oxygen."

Lombardi not only struggled with a violent temper, he also had a tendency at times to be impatient, insensitive, unkind, and even cruel. Those moments usually occurred when he was in the heat of a practice or when someone said something that caught him off guard. He then would react with an emotional, shoot-from-the-hip type of response—a shout, a blurting out of something, an insult. After a while, though, Vince would regret what he had just said or done. Then he'd begin to feel bad. And next, in order to live with himself, he would go and apologize.

This pattern—of *bad behavior, regret, feeling bad, apology*—is similar to that of children who cannot control themselves. But with Vince Lombardi, it happened throughout his entire career. When he was an assistant coach with the New York Giants, for example, Vince had to apologize during a practice to running back Eddie Price, who became so disgusted with Lombardi's verbal abuse that he yelled, "Enough of this! I'm quitting the game." When Price took off for the clubhouse, Vince, according to an assistant coach, "went running after him like a little puppy dog, yelling, 'Eddie, Eddie, come back; come back!'" Another time, when Vince was head coach for the Packers, he once got so disgusted with a rookie that he screamed out in frustration: "You're not only big and fat; you're stupid, too!" The rookie was cut after that practice. However, Lombardi, knowing that he had said something terrible, kept thinking about it until he finally left the office in time to catch the rookie boarding a bus for home. "I'm sorry, son," said Vince. "I had no right to embarrass you like that when you had no chance of making the team."

Over his career, people have noted, Vince frequently said things like: "I'm selfish," "I did something I'm sorry for," or, "I made a mistake." This constant apologizing for something he had done wrong is a revealing facet of Lombardi's character. Clearly, he had to make amends more than the average person. However, the frequency of his apologies tends to indicate that Lombardi had a healthy dose of both compassion and self-worth. Not only did he not want to intentionally hurt people, but he was also not afraid to look bad by admitting he was wrong. Many men will not say they're sorry for *anything*—or even *think* of apologizing. They will not do it because they feel that it might make them look bad or eat into their machismo. But Vince Lombardi had few such thoughts. When he realized he had done something wrong, he said he was sorry—and he did so either in private or in front of the entire team, whichever was necessary. It happened many times.

However, just as a no-nonsense mother will sometimes say to her repentant child, " 'Sorry' won't cut it this time!," Lombardi's apologies only went so far with his players. Kicking a wastebasket into Jerry Kramer's chair, pounding on wide receiver Steve Wright's chest, telling Jim Taylor that "I made you, mister, and you're nothing without me," and insulting center Ken Bowman (who was studying for a law degree in the off-season) by saying, "You're too stupid to play this game, let alone become a lawyer!" are just a few examples of how Vince Lombardi mistreated members of his football teams. Such behavior not only tends to grate on players' nerves; it also serves to bring out a plethora of negative reactions and emotions that no leader can long afford to have festering in his teams.

First of all, it *frightens* people. As one man who played for Lombardi said: "It's a terrible feeling to know you're afraid of the man you work for, terrible."

Second, it causes a *resentment* that can sometimes lead to mocking behavior. "He was tough and abusive and at times he was downright nasty," said Bart Starr, one of Lombardi's favorites—and Bart Starr never said anything bad about anyone. "I swear he preached humility to enhance his own ego!" Max McGee once exclaimed in ridicule.

Third, such behavior causes people to be unusually *argumentative*, which, of course, can be disruptive to team unity and discipline. New

York Giant coach Jim Lee Howell never forgot the time Vince yelled at a player for messing up a play when the guy snapped back, "I think the heat's got you." "Well you can imagine!" exclaimed Howell. "Vince ended up chasing the player down the field."

Fourth, abusive behavior by a leader engenders what is perhaps the worst of all human emotions—*hate*. "At times, I couldn't stand the sight of him," said Bill Curry. "I hated him for [screaming at me] in front of everyone," said Fuzzy Thurston. "I hate this son of a bitch," many players would say behind his back.

Finally, some people will refuse to work for such a leader. Star running back Bob Brunet, for example, simply walked out of Redskin training camp one afternoon and refused to return. And one of Lombardi's assistant coaches, Bill Austin, resigned after spending five years with the Packers. "He was such a domineering man," said Austin of Lombardi. "After a while, it gets you. I just had to get away."

Vince Lombardi was well aware of his darker side. "Like my father before me," he said, "I have a violent temper with which I have been struggling all my life . . . I don't understand it—I never use bad language until I get to the football season. . . . My ego just can't accept a loss. . . . I'm restless, worrisome, demanding, sometimes impatient and hot-tempered. . . . I've got all the emotions in excess and a hair trigger controls them. I anger and I laugh and I cry quickly, and so I couldn't have told you five minutes later what else I said or just what I did."

He also knew that such negative elements of his personal character could be extraordinarily detrimental to a person in his profession. So he constantly sought to keep his emotions under control. Having been raised a good Catholic boy, he sought to control himself was by attending mass. But Lombardi didn't just go to mass once in a while or once a week—he went *every single day*. When he coached the Washington Redskins, for instance, Vince would wake up at six o'clock each morning and attend the 7:00 A.M. service at Our Lady of Mercy Catholic Church near his home. Or he might first make the drive to the Redskins' offices and then attend the 7:30 mass at St. Matthew's Cathedral. Either way, whenever the team was in town, Vince first went to church before interacting with his team. "I have such a terrible temper," he once told a friend, "it's the only way I can keep it under control."

This was a pattern of behavior that occurred throughout Lombardi's entire professional coaching career. As a matter of fact, in 1959 Bart Starr picked up some scuttlebutt that his new coach was a man who worshiped every day. "When I heard about this man taking over the team, I could hardly wait to meet a man that went to church every day," remembered Starr. "I worked for him two weeks and then I realized that this man *needs* to go to church every day!"

In addition to working very hard to control his emotions, Vince consciously employed a variety of actions (such as frequent apologies) designed to offset or diffuse the negative emotions that invariably arose when he *did* lose his cool. He often injected humor, for instance, whenever he sensed that a mood change might help. A good example occurred when Max McGee was given a speeding ticket by the Wisconsin State Patrol late at night—while he was out breaking the team's curfew. The incident appeared in the newspaper the next morning, and Lombardi was so angry at the team meeting that he was shaking.

"Max," he screamed, "that'll cost you five hundred bucks! If you go again, it'll cost you a thousand!" The room fell deathly silent and you could cut the tension with a knife. Then Vince calmed down, stopped shaking, and a slight smile crossed his face. "Max," he said gently, "if you can find anything worth sneaking out for, for a thousand bucks, hell, call me and I'll go with you." The place then erupted in laughter and Vince had managed to lighten the moment considerably. "Oh, he'd get furious," remembered Frank Gifford. "But then he'd laugh right along with the rest of us."

Another mechanism Lombardi employed was to immediately praise or, at the very least, offer some kind words to the person he might have just offended. When Packer public relations director Tom Miller angrily snapped back at his boss after being yelled at, Vince complimented Miller and, later that day, gave him a $1,000 bonus check.

Another time, veteran Emlen Tunnell was accused by Lombardi of not hustling during practice. "All right, Emlen," he said in front of the entire team, "you don't want to play, just get off the field. Get out of here!" Tunnell stalked off the field both hurt and angry. The next morning, Lombardi walked into the dressing room and, in front of the entire team, went right up to Tunnell and said, "Emlen, you mad at me?"

"Damn right I am," came the terse reply. "You acted like a high school coach. Heck, I didn't do anything wrong. The ball was out-of-bounds. I was hustling."

Then Lombardi winked, offered a handshake, and asked, "We still friends?"

"It took a big man to come to me like that," Emlen remarked later. "A helluva big man. He didn't have to do that. Boy, that was all I ever needed—just a little wink from him, a little kind word—and it made all the work worthwhile."

In general, there were two other things that enabled Vince's players to tolerate and accept the darker aspects of his personality. First, Lombardi won football games. As Fuzzy Thurston once so aptly described after being yelled at for four straight hours in a film session: "I hated him that day. I hated him right up till the next Sunday when we killed the Los Angeles Rams." Second, Lombardi opened up and showed people his better side—the loving, the caring, and the compassionate aspects of his personality. In short, it is extremely important for leaders to take note of the fact that if Vince Lombardi had not won football games—and if his players had not truly believed that he loved and cared about them—then he wouldn't have lasted more than a single season as their leader. He would have been gone.

To the people on his team, Lombardi was a man of many contradictions. He confused them by alternating between kindness and abuse. "He made you feel like a million bucks right after you felt like two cents a minute before," remembered one player. Because his moods swung from deep depression to soaring exhilaration, they called him Mr. High-Low. "He was either smiling or he was frowning," commented another. "I wonder which Vince we're going to see today," the players and staff wondered upon arriving at work each morning. They observed a man who was loud and gregarious but also shy and insecure; who preached both hate for his opponents and love for his fellow man; who showed great humility and yet had a soaring ego; who spoke in kind, soothing tones one minute and, in the next, swore like a man with Tourette's syndrome. "It was religion in the morning and the language of the longshoreman in the afternoon," said a Packer assistant coach.

And just as Lombardi exuded a variety of mixed signals and contradictory emotions, so did the players have deep-seated mixed emotions about *him*. "It's hard to resist hating him, his ranting, his raving, his screaming, his hollering. But, damn him, he's a great coach!" said Jerry Kramer. "As a man, I didn't like him, but as a coach, he was the greatest," said Ken Bowman. "As much as I hated the guy, and I did, I hated him," remembered lineman Ray Schoenke, "I had tremendous respect for him, tremendous. I played some of the best football of my life under him. It's a paradox."

And that's exactly what Vince Lombardi was to everybody: a paradox, an enigma—difficult, if not impossible, to understand. Even his own wife could not totally figure him out. "He's kind of a mystery," said Marie. "He eludes you."

But oddly enough, one of Vince Lombardi's greatest faults also tended to be one of his greatest assets. Red Blaik noted so when he stated that Vince's temper "was so extreme that it would awaken the participants and create a certain amount of fear in the individual." And Lombardi himself both intuitively and strategically sought to make his extreme emotions work *for* him. "You can't be a cold fish and go out and coach," he said. "If you're going to be involved in it, you gotta take your emotions with you. . . ."

"It is this temper," he went on to say, "that keeps me on edge and allows me to get things done and people to do things. . . . It is ineradicable, but it must not be irrational. I coach with everything that is within me, and I employ that temper for a purpose."

Football players had to accept the total package if they wanted to win. They had to accept the fact that with Vince Lombardi life was going to be experienced to the fullest; that they were going to come into contact with virtually every emotion life had to offer—happiness and sadness, exhilaration and depression, love and hate, all of them. That was part of the price they had to pay for being champions.

But perhaps life with Lombardi was toughest of all for members of his immediate family—for his son, Vince Jr., for his daughter, Susan, and for his wife, Marie. Their internal struggles in dealing with such a force of a man had to have been supremely difficult.

Even though she had her difficult moments, Marie had the resilience to handle and adapt to Vince over the years, a fact that sheds light on her own personal integrity and character. She would not always comply with her husband's demands. She would stand up to him and put him in his place when needed—which, paradoxically, Vince admired rather than resented.

And Marie Lombardi knew when to call in the cavalry for help.

About a week before her husband was due to report to the Washington Redskin training camp for the very first time—after a year-long layoff from coaching—she made a call to Lombardi's close friend Ockie Krueger.

"Ockie, what are you doing right now?" Marie asked.

"Nothing," he replied.

"Well get over here quick and let's go out for dinner," she pleaded. "Vince has started cleaning out the closets again."

Lombardi Principles

- When you do something wrong, you should apologize—not only to make amends but also to live with yourself.
- The ability to apologize indicates that you have a healthy dose of both compassion and self-worth.
- Remember that apologies, no matter how sincere, only go so far in placating the members of your team.
- Continued abusive behavior frightens people, causes resentment, leads to arguments, engenders hate, and causes people to quit and walk away.
- Seek to keep your emotions under control.
- Employ a variety of actions that offset or diffuse the negative emotions that are caused when you lose your cool.
- Inject some humor whenever you sense that a mood change will help the team.
- After you've lost your temper and possibly insulted someone, immediately come back and praise the individual or, at the very least, offer some kind words—or a wink and a handshake.
- If your darker side comes through too often, you had better win ball games and make sure the players believe that you love and care about them. Otherwise, you'll be gone.
- You can't be a cold fish and go out and lead. If you're going to be involved, you have to take your emotions with you.
- Coach with everything that is within you. If you have a bad temper, employ it for a purpose.

We all have to have a little love for each other. If you don't have it, forget it. . . . Love is the answer to everything.

VINCE LOMBARDI

He said, "Look, here's air fare for Bobby and I don't ever want to hear anything else about this."

WILLIE DAVIS,
ON COACH LOMBARDI

Heart power is the strength of the Green Bay Packers. Heart power is the strength of America, and hate power is the weakness of the world.

VINCE LOMBARDI

18 Preach Love, Family, and Heart Power

On the afternoon of February 10, 1967, Jerry Kramer stopped by the Packers' office to pick up his mail. It was only three weeks after Green Bay's big victory in Super Bowl I, and he expected everybody to still be in a joyous and festive mood. So it surprised him no end to see a forlorn-looking Vince Lombardi emerging from the building.

"Hi, Coach," said a concerned Kramer.

Lombardi opened his mouth, but no words came out. He hung his head in despair, then tried once more to speak. But, again, he was still too emotional to say even one word.

"What is it, Coach?" asked Kramer, who now realized something dreadfully serious had taken place. "What's the matter?"

At last, Vince choked out a few words: "I had to put Paul . . . I had to put Paul on that list. And they took him."

Kramer just stood there looking incredulous. He realized that Lombardi was talking about having placed Paul Hornung on the draft list for the National Football League's new expansion team, the New Orleans

Saints. And to Vince's shock, the Saints had selected Horning. Now it was Kramer who could not find words to respond.

"This is a helluva business sometimes, isn't it?" said Lombardi as he turned and walked away.

For a week or more afterward, Vince became emotional when he had to speak about the loss of Hornung to the Saints. He hadn't placed Paul on the list to lose him, he explained to friends. Paul was at the end of his career. It didn't make sense for New Orleans to take him. It was a good strategy. He had to protect younger Packer players. He had to do it for the good of the team.

Many people who observed Lombardi's anguish assumed he had been particularly affected because he felt closer to Hornung than he did to most players. And clearly, that was part of it. "[Paul] was more like a son to me," Vince admitted. But as Jerry Kramer would write that same year, "We are all Lombardi's sons, his children."

The players, almost to a man, viewed Vince as "a parent figure" or "a father image." When he chastised them, it was "like a father scolding a son," said one. When they were preparing for a game in New York, "he warned us about all the evils of the big city," said another. "He thinks of himself as the patriarch of a large family," explained Kramer, "and he loves all his children, and he worries about all of them. . . ."

Lombardi frequently mentioned the notion of family when talking about his team. "There's a great, great closeness on a football team," he said. "a rapport between the men and the coach that's like no other sport. It's a binding together, a knitting together. For me, it's like father and sons." And like a conscientious father with his sons, Lombardi always tried to talk straight with them. He cared enough to tell them the truth, whether the truth hurt or not. A case in point involved tight end Ron Kramer. When Vince first took over the Packers, Kramer was not performing up to either his reputation or his ability. "He was falling on his face," observed Lombardi. "His legs were bad and his attitude was worse. [We] carried him in 1959 and 1960."

At the beginning of the 1961 season, Vince called Ron into his office and had a one-on-one conversation to explain the hard facts. "I told him I would start him in every preseason game," said Lombardi, "but that if he didn't come through for us he was done." That session seemed to wake up Kramer, because almost immediately his performance improved and, eventually, he regained his old form and became a star in the National Football League.

But all of Lombardi's heart-to-heart chats did not have the desired effect. One year the Packers drafted a six-one 240-pound lineman from a top university. The rookie not only had the "physical toughness" Lombardi was always looking for, but he also was a straight-A student with "a fine mind." However, as Vince quickly recognized, this young man "broke down mentally in every game and even in practice. He simply did not have a football mentality. He wouldn't pull when he was supposed to pull or he'd block the wrong man." So Lombardi sat the rookie down, explained what he had observed, and then asked: "Can you tell me what's the matter?"

"I don't know," came the dejected response. "I just don't know."

After that conversation, Lombardi used the kid sporadically and monitored his progress. But in a preseason game against the Detroit Lions, a mistake by the rookie let 270-pound Alex Karras "barrel in and almost kill Bart Starr." "I thought it was the end of my team," Lombardi gasped.

The next morning, when the coaches were viewing game film of the play, Vince asked Bill Austin what the rookie had done wrong—even though he already knew the answer. Starr had called an audible at the line of scrimmage and changed from a running play to a passing play, explained Austin. The rookie had missed it. He had obviously "pulled" instead of "pass-blocked."

"I'm sorry," said Lombardi, "but he's gone."

And Vince really was sorry. He found it very difficult to tell anyone that he had not made the team, which, as every coach knows, usually means four out of five players who try out. One year, Lombardi had to give the bad news to a young man "who was hoping to support four younger brothers and sisters by playing pro ball." Another year, he had to tell a rookie who had been trying very hard but just couldn't make the grade. The kid broke down crying. "That's when you ache inside," said Vince, who often commented that this was the hardest part of his job.

It was so hard for Lombardi, in fact, that he finally delegated the duty of cutting rookies to Pat Peppler, the Packers' director of player personnel. "He was too kindhearted to fire anyone," said Tom Miller. "If people were cut, there was no explanation," remembered one veteran. "They were just gone. The locker next door would be empty—like the guy had disappeared into thin air." The truth is that Vince Lombardi just did not like to talk about letting people go because it was too emotional for him to discuss.

Lombardi had a particularly tough time informing his veteran players when their time had come to retire—a task that he *did not* delegate, because of the closeness he had with them. In Vince's mind, it just would just not have been right to allow a veteran to be let go without hearing about it from him personally. When Emlen Tunnell got to that point, both men knew it was time. But that didn't prevent Lombardi from crying like a baby when the two sat down to discuss it. Emlen, however, was not surprised that his coach cried. He had seen it before, as had all of Lombardi's players and close friends. "If you said good morning to him in the right way," said Wellington Mara, "you could bring tears to his eyes." "Hell, I'm an emotional man," explained Vince. "I cry . . . I'm not ashamed of crying."

On occasion, in the team locker room after an important victory, Lombardi would be moved to tears at the effort his players had put forth. "All right," he'd say, "that was a great team effort! It was . . ." Then his voice would break, his eyes would well up, his lips would tremble, and his whole body would quiver. Finally, Lombardi would just stand there, in the middle of the room surrounded by his team, with tears streaming down his cheeks.

When this happened the players would begin to cheer to take some of the pressure off their coach. At that moment, Lombardi would kneel down and, still fighting to get words out, lead the team in the Lord's Prayer—and thank God that no one had been seriously injured.

After the prayer, Vince was more composed. "Okay! I'm all right now," he'd say. "Have your fun now. You deserve it. We'll get down to work again on Tuesday. That's all."

One memorable day, Vince surprised the Packers by beginning his locker-room remarks with a question that most of them had never before heard come from the mouth of a football coach.

"What is the meaning of love?" he asked. "Anybody can love something that is beautiful or smart or agile. You will never know love until you can love something that isn't beautiful, isn't bright, isn't glamorous. It takes a special person to love something unattractive, someone unknown. That is the test of love. Everybody can love someone's strengths and good looks. But can you like somebody's weaknesses? Can you accept him for his inabilities? That's what we have to do. That's what love is."

After that brief opening, Vince then related his concept of brotherly love directly to each individual as they might experience it on the playing field. "You might have a guy playing next to you who maybe isn't perfect," Vince said, "but you've got to love him, and maybe that love would enable you to help him. And maybe you will do something more to overcome a difficult situation in football because of that love."

This locker-room episode was not a onetime thing. There were other occasions when Lombardi preached love to his team on an idealistic, even esoteric basis. "I am not advocating a love which forces everyone to love the white man because he is white or the black man because he is black or the poor because he is poor or your enemy because he is your enemy," he once said. "But rather of a love that one man has for another human being, any human being who happens to be white or black, rich or poor, enemy or friend."

And Lombardi frequently mentioned love in relation to his concept of mental toughness, which, again, got right back to relating the subject directly to the football playing field: "The love I'm speaking of is not necessarily liking, or the love that a man may have for his wife. The love I'm speaking of is loyalty, which is the greatest of loves. Teamwork, the love that one man has for another and that he respects the dignity of another. The love I'm speaking of is charity."

In addition to talking about love and charity, Vince put his money where his mouth was. In fact, his friends worried that he was too much of a soft touch, because he constantly donated large amounts of money to charitable organizations—especially those managed by the Catholic church. Frequently he would give a speech and then immediately turn around and contribute the honorarium to a charitable institution. After one speech, he gave $5,000 to a student scholarship fund. After a talk in New York City, he asked a close friend to give his $2,500 check to Fordham University. And immediately following a talk in Atlantic City, New Jersey, he stopped by a convent on the way home and signed his check over to a nun.

Lombardi was also extraordinarily active with nonprofit organizations, lending out his name and his time generously. In Wisconsin, he was a member of the Citizens Committee of St. Norbert College, president of Wisconsin's Mental Health Association, chairman of the Wisconsin City of Hope Leukemia Drive, chairman of the State's Cancer Fund, cochairman of the Governor's Council on Physical Fitness, director of Pop Warner Football, and a member of the Council for Human Relations in Green Bay. In Washington, D.C., he served on the advisory board of the National Capital Area Council of the Boy Scouts of America, was a member of the board of trustees of the District of Columbia Division of the American Cancer Society, on the Committee for Children's Hospital of the District of Columbia, and honorary chairman of the Washington Kidney Foundation Drive, to name a few of his activities.

When asked about why he was so involved in charitable work, Vince would invariably give a reply that revealed his deeply compassionate nature. "We are our brother's keeper," he said to one audience. "If people can't find work, whether it's their fault or not, you've got to help them, clothe them, and house them properly and try to get rid of the conditions that have held them back." To another group, he said simply: "If there must be wrinkles upon our brow, let them not be on our heart."

Understanding Vince Lombardi's compassionate nature is key to unlocking the mystery of his exceptional leadership ability—because it was, in part, *precisely* this deep-rooted compassion that gave Vince the ability to inspire others to perform better than they ever thought they could.

Lombardi cared enough to think seriously about all things that impacted his players. "The members of a team must constantly have their needs considered," he explained. "Players think constantly of continuity and regularity of employment, adequate compensation and recognition, satisfactory working conditions, a sense of secure belonging, and pride in their work and their organization." Therefore, a leader, according to Lombardi, "must be sensitive to the emotional needs and expectations of others. In return, the attitude toward him should be one of confidence and, possibly, affection."

Vince not only thought about the players themselves; he also constantly considered the problems their families might be going through—and then he sought to do what he could to ease their burdens. "A professional football team is a kind of community of displaced persons," he pointed out when he was with the Packers. "A few of them and their families live in the Green Bay area the year around, but the rest are here only from July through December. When the first-year men are single or newly married it is comparatively simple to find them apartments, but as their families grow through the years it is a problem to find them suitable houses and there is a mad scramble every summer. They come from all over the country and some of the wives have never before left the towns where they were born. Often they are homesick and unhappy with local customs or local climate."

This statement is revealing not only for Lombardi's detailed knowledge of his players and their families but also for the fact that he felt it was part of his duty as the head coach to help them find suitable living arrangements. "In the three years I was in Green Bay," recalled Emlen Tunnell (who initially could not find a place to stay because he was African-American), "[Coach Lombardi] picked up my hotel bill at the Northland. He didn't have to do that."

Nor did Lombardi have to show as much concern as he showed or render the many kindnesses he did—things like: inquiring about the condition of running back Earl Gros's wife after she had surgery; calling Henry Jordan at the hospital to ask how his young son, Butch, was after having broken his leg; inviting another player, his wife, and two sons over for Christmas dinner when their small daughter was confined to a hospital bed with pneumonia; boarding Assistant Coach Tom Fears's son in his home for four months until Fears could find a house and move his family in, and paying the air fare for cornerback Bob Jeter to attend the funeral of a relative. "Look," said Lombardi, handing the money to Willie Davis to pass on to Jeter, "here's the money for Bobby and I don't ever want to hear anything else about this."

Despite the fact that Vince usually did not talk about these many small acts of kindness, word quickly got around. And after a while, people began to feel so attached to Vince Lombardi and the Green Bay Packers team environment that some were apprehensive that it would all end. "The fear is simple," explained Willie Davis. "It's just the plain, frightening idea that something will prevent you from remaining a part of this." Linebacker Bill Forrester said he actually reached a point where he wanted his teammates to receive more credit then himself—something that most people only feel about their immediate families. "We had as much unity as you possibly could have," remembered Jim Taylor, "which goes along with the love aspect he always talked about." Even Lombardi himself answered a reporter after the victory in Super Bowl I that the primary reason for the success of the Green Bay Packers was, quite simply, "Love." "There is love on this ball club," he said.

Vince's innate compassion and quiet kindness not only served to instill trust in players but also tended to offset the players' negative reactions to Lombardi's usually gruff persona. "He had a hard exterior," noted Ray Nitschke, "but he also had a big, soft heart."

And it was that heart that made all the difference in the world.

A heart that was true and genuine.

A heart that Lombardi wore not only on his sleeve but also on the Super Bowl ring he personally designed—with the words CHARACTER on one side of the center stone and LOVE on the other.

Vince Lombardi's was a shining heart whose brilliance could be seen at any given moment of the day. It glowed in a crowd and it twinkled when he was alone.

"One time I went shopping with my daughter Suzanne, who was then an infant, and a baby-sitter," related Henry Jordan's wife, Olive. "I was driving an old car we had, and I left Suzanne and the baby-sitter in the car when I ran into the store. When I came out, the baby-sitter told me that Suzanne had been at the window, smiling and waving at everyone, and a man had come down the street and waved back and walked up to the window and smiled at Suzanne. And the baby-sitter almost fainted, because the man was Lombardi. He didn't recognize the car, because it wasn't Henry's, and he didn't recognize Suzanne, because he couldn't know all the players' children, and, of course, he didn't recognize the baby-sitter. But he had compassion for a little baby waving to him, and he wanted to make sure that he didn't hurt her feelings."

"Heart power is the strength of the Green Bay Packers," said Vince Lombardi. "Heart power is the strength of America, and hate power is the weakness of the world."

Lombardi Principles

- Think of yourself as the patriarch of a large family who loves all his children and worries about them.
- Talk straight with the members of your team. Care enough about them to tell them the truth.
- It is not right to let a veteran player go without first speaking to him personally.
- Do not be ashamed of crying.
- You will never know love until you can love something that isn't beautiful, isn't bright, isn't glamorous. That is the true test of love.
- Loving an individual who isn't perfect may help you overcome a difficult personal situation.
- Remember that love is the answer to everything.
- Donate your time, money, and name to worthy causes.
- If there must be wrinkles upon your brow, let them not be in your heart.
- Be sensitive to the emotional needs and expectations of others. In return, the attitude toward you should be one of confidence and, possibly, affection.
- Show concern for your players and their families. Render small acts of kindness.
- Remember, heart power is the strength of your organization.

*Whatever the job we have, we must pay a price for success. It's like any-
thing worthwhile. It has a price. You have to pay the price to win and you
have to pay the price to get to the point where success is possible. Most
important, you must pay the price to stay there.*

VINCE LOMBARDI

*There are three things that are important to every man in this room.
His religion, his family, and the Green Bay Packers, in that order.*

VINCE LOMBARDI,
IN HIS FIRST MEETING WITH THE PACKERS

Success demands singleness of purpose.
VINCE LOMBARDI

19 — Be Willing to Pay the Price for Success

"Don't forget me!" said Susan Lombardi, snapping her dad out of his
trance.

Every morning, as her father drove her to school on his way to the
office, Vince's daughter had to remind him to drop her off. If she didn't
speak up, he would invariably miss his turn and drive right by the high
school—sometimes miles by. It wasn't so much that Lombardi was for-
getful; it's just that his mind was totally consumed with football. Other
than Susan's reminder, nothing but a lone traffic light, as Vince noted,
"invades my consciousness [and] consistently interrupts that single purpose of winning next Sunday's game."

All week long, Lombardi's total focus was on that next football game.
His concentration was so encompassing that it seemed to exclude all
other things, including even the most mundane and normal habits of
everyday life. Marie Lombardi, for instance, recalled the time that Vince
"parked his car three driveways down from ours and walked into a
neighbor's house." Bill Austin never forgot when, after a practice ses-

sion, "Vince showered and put on his socks and his shirt and his shoes and his jacket and his overcoat and started to walk out of the stadium. The man at the gate stopped him. 'Excuse me, Mr. Lombardi,' he said, 'but I think you should go back and put your pants on.'" And then there was the time that an assistant coach (subbing for Marie) drove Vince to the train station. When they arrived, Lombardi said, "Thanks, honey," kissed the coach on the cheek, and then got on the train. "He never knew he did it," recalled the assistant.

Outside of football, Vince had very few interests or hobbies. He played golf occasionally but always felt guilty for having done so. He didn't spend time doing yard work or fixing up his house—not even so much as changing a burned-out lightbulb. Rather, he concentrated on his job—to the exclusion of everything else—because, as far as he was concerned, nothing else mattered.

Employees, players, and reporters tended to get miffed when Lombardi walked by them in the halls without acknowledging their presence. "I'd walk by and say, 'Good morning, sir,'—and he'd say, 'Harrumph,' like a bear," complained one person. "Forget it," advised an assistant coach. "He's thinking of Sunday, nothing else." And the Packers' chief scout, Wally Cruice, pointed out that "you didn't talk about anything but football. If you didn't have the facts, he didn't want you to waste his time."

Eventually, though, everybody got used to Lombardi's idiosyncrasies—and they also accepted the fact that nothing would prevent him from preparing his team for their upcoming game. Nothing—not even the Cuban Missile Crisis of 1962, when Green Bay had a practice scheduled during President Kennedy's deadline for the Russians and Cubans to dismantle their nuclear missiles. If the deadline was not met, the United States would be going to war.

"We were all pretty anxious," remembered Jerry Kramer, "and somebody suggested to Vince that we postpone or cancel the workout."

"The hell with Cuba!" roared Lombardi. "Let's go to work!"

"We won the NFL championship that year," recalled Kramer.

From mid-July through the end of the football season (which sometimes went to January if the Packers made it to the title game), Vince concentrated on his job and almost never took a day off. But far from the average person's eight-hour work day, Lombardi devoted sixteen to eighteen hours a day to his job.

He would rise at 6:00 every morning and be one of the first people to arrive at the office. He'd usually drive home for dinner at 5:30 P.M., but then return to work and stay until 10:00 or 11:00 at night. Traveling to and from the office, Vince would carry an old briefcase or a thick notebook stuffed with papers. At home, he kept an updated file cabinet with all his diagrammed plays and personal coaching notes.

He was always thinking about his football team—always. And predictably, Lombardi's family had to do without him for most of the year. "Come football season, I may as well kiss him good-bye," his wife once told a friend. As a matter of fact, Marie swore that she could tell what day of the week it was just by observing the kind of mood he was in. "Monday, Tuesday, and Wednesday, we didn't talk. Thursday, we said hello. Friday, he was civil, and Saturday, he was downright pleasant. Sunday, he was relaxed most of the day."

Monday was devoted to reviewing films of the previous day's game—usually from 9:00 A.M. to 5:00 P.M. Then Vince would tape his Packer television show and go back to the office for another three or four hours. On Tuesday, all day was spent with the players—again reviewing the game films, meticulously going over every individual's performance, beginning to plan for next Sunday's upcoming opponent, and then hitting the practice field. "For every hour of game play that we put in," noted Lombardi, "we put in fourteen on those [practice] fields. . . . And then there are those hours spent in meetings—the time we coaches spend in preparation for those practice sessions and those meetings."

If everything was going well in Vince's mind, he and the other coaches might get Thursday night off to spend with their families. If not, they'd all be at the office grinding out a better plan. About that time every week Lombardi could use a night off, because his voice started to get hoarse from all the talking during meetings and yelling during practices. But by the weekend, he actually began to lighten up a little bit. "Driving into town, I am aware of the scenes around me for the first time in a week," he said, describing his Saturday commute to the office.

Predictably, Vince Lombardi's workaholic approach to his job had a tremendous impact on everyone associated with the Green Bay Packers—players, staff, and coaches. He not only told the team at their very first meeting that he expected "a one-hundred-percent effort at all times," and that "anything less than that is not good enough," but he also informed everybody of their new priorities.

"There are three things that are important to every man in this room," he said. "His religion, his family, and the Green Bay Packers, in that order." He wanted his players and coaches to have no other outside interests, no "extracurricular whatnot," as he phrased it. "If a man's performance falls off," Lombardi theorized, "possibly he has misdirected his attention to something far less essential than his job." And to reinforce his point, Vince would lecture the team over and over and over again—and sometimes not in the most pleasant manner.

"I want every minute of your day to be devoted to football," he demanded at one practice. "This is the only thing you're here for." A moment later, after someone on the offensive squad missed a key block, Lombardi exploded. "Who was supposed to be on that man?" he asked.

"I was," confessed Fuzzy Thurston.

"WHAT IN THE HELL IS GOING ON HERE?" Lombardi screamed. "What in the hell are you thinking about? You've got too many restaurants, too much hunting, too many outside interests. I've had it. I'm disgusted with you guys. The hell with you. Let's go to defense. The hell with the offense. You guys can stick it in your diddy bag."

And then there was the time that Assistant Coach Red Cochran made the mistake of asking to go home a little early on a Wednesday night. It was the week before Christmas 1960, and the Packers were preparing for their NFL championship game against the Philadelphia Eagles.

"Coach, is there any chance of getting off before nine o'clock tonight? Maybe eight-thirty," asked Cochran. "I could do a little Christmas shopping before the stores close."

"Red, you wanna be Santa Claus or you wanna be a football coach?" Lombardi responded. "There's no room for both!"

"Success," according to Vince Lombardi, was "not a sometime thing," but "an all-time thing." It could be attained if "you work better and harder than the next guy," if you had a "singleness of purpose" that "enables you to ignore the minor hurts, the opponent's pressure, and the temporary failures." There were no shortcuts to success, he believed. "The individual who tries to find them will lose his way." Rather, a man could be as great as he wanted to be if he was willing to "sacrifice the little things in life," and pay the price for "the things that are worthwhile."

"Whatever the job we have, we must pay a price for success," Lombardi frequently told his team. "It's like anything worthwhile. It has a price. You have to pay the price to win and you have to pay the price to get to the point where success is possible. Most important, you must pay the price to stay there."

Staying on top was a particularly tough challenge, as Lombardi and the Packers found out after they won back-to-back championships in 1961 and 1962 but then missed the play-offs the next two years. When Lombardi was asked why they had failed, he said: "We're all to blame—the newspapers, the team, the coaches, and the people. Nobody got a kick out of winning anymore, or even scoring a touchdown. When we won a close game, people would wonder why we didn't win by a bigger score—or get more touchdowns. Gradually, there was less emotion, less elation with winning." Success made everybody "fatheaded," according to Vince. The players' egos "overwhelmed them," and "they were no longer willing to pay the price."

But no one could say that was true of Lombardi. Every single player and coach realized the tremendous amount of time, heart, and passion he put into his job. "You have to pay a price for victory, and the coach paid more than his share," noted Ray Nitschke. "I believe he works harder than any man I've ever known," observed Jerry Kramer. "He demands more of himself and his assistant coaches than anyone in the league." And far from intimidating people, Lombardi's work ethic actually inspired the best players on the team. "He worked so hard that I always felt the old man was really putting more into the game on a day-to-day basis than I was," remembered Willie Davis. "I felt obligated to put something extra into it on Sunday."

Part of the price Vince Lombardi paid was, quite simply, the price every leader has to pay for being a leader. He had to make the tough decisions when others were reluctant to do so. He had to fire players to whom he'd become quite attached, for instance. "Football coaches are usually reluctant to change a successful team," he said, "[but] there's no room for that emotion . . . If a player isn't as good as he was last year when he won the championship for you, he's got to go."

Veteran All-Pro defensive lineman Sam Huff found that out in a most unusual way. In 1969, Huff came out of retirement at Lombardi's request and, as a player-coach, helped lead the Washington Redskins to their first winning season in fifteen years. "At the end of the season," Huff remembered, "we were sitting one day, all the coaches watching the films, and Vince jumped up and pointed at the screen and hollered, 'That number seventy's to slow! He's not moving fast enough! We've got to get a new man in there!' That's when I knew it was time for me to retire again," said Huff. "I was number seventy."

As far as Vince Lombardi, the leader, was concerned, no one could be carried. *Everyone* had to contribute. "There are no spectators," he said, "only players."

Leadership can also be a lonely job. That was clearly another price Vince paid for being a head coach. "There weren't many people like him," remembered Lionel Aldridge, "nobody to hang out with who was like him. In that sense, I think he might have been lonely. He was a one-class warrior, a one-trick pony in that he had one way of doing things—his way—and it was the right way."

There was also the price Lombardi paid by letting his family take a backseat to his job. He was constantly forgetting his wedding anniversary, for instance. In 1965, Vince's wife had scheduled a twenty-fifth-anniversary celebration but angrily canceled it after she found out that her husband had scheduled a Packer team meeting for the same night. "I was fool enough to be married during the football season," lamented Marie. But as Jim Taylor recalled, "Marie must have chewed him out good, [because] for the next two or three days, he took it all out on us. He was miserable. We all went and wrote down his anniversary so that we could remind him in case he ever forgot again."

Finally, Vince seemed to wear down from the tremendous energy it took to maintain his particular level of dedication. Toward the end of his tenure with the Packers, he frequently mentioned things like: "I feel a little tired," or, "It's the constant grind; you just wear out," or, "It's been a long time since I've had a day off."

Inevitably, though, he would bounce back. "My heart tells me to lie down and take a rest," he'd say, "but I don't do it. I keep going from early in the morning until late at night."

Vince Lombardi believed that "leaders are made; they are not born" and "they are made by *hard effort*." He also believed that leadership is "in sacrifice," "in self-denial," "in love," "in fearlessness," "in humility," and "in the perfectly disciplined will." "This is the distinction between great and little men," he said.

That's why Lombardi would wake up at 3:25 most Monday mornings, not "sleeping the sleep of the victor," as he said, "but wide awake, seeing the other people who are coming in next Sunday."

That's why, after a long hard day of work, he would drive back to the office after dinner, take off his coat, and say to his assistants: "All right, let's start enumerating those defenses."

Lombardi Principles

- Let nothing prevent you from preparing your team for the upcoming contest.
- If everything is going well, give everybody some time off. If not, get in there and grind out a better plan.
- Expect 100 percent effort at all times. Anything less than that is not good enough.
- Cut back on the extracurricular whatnot.
- If a man's performance falls off, possibly he has misdirected his attention to something far less essential than his job.
- Success demands singleness of purpose. It is not a sometime thing; it is an all-the-time thing.
- There are no shortcuts to success. The individual who tries to find them will lose his way.
- The team must somehow get the feeling that there is a dedication coming from the top and it must be worth something.
- Whatever job you have, you have to pay a price for success.
- Far from intimidating people, a hard work ethic actually inspires the best players on your team.
- Leaders have to make the tough decisions that others are unwilling to make.
- There are no spectators, only players.
- It can be done.

The quality of a man's life has got to be a full measure of that man's personal commitment to excellence and victory, regardless of what field he may be in.

VINCE LOMBARDI

Vince developed character in his players, character that a lot of them probably would never have had without [his] leadership. Therefore, they never were out of the game. They never felt like there wasn't some hope. And that is what carried them through to that third championship. That is what beat us.

TOM LANDRY,
ON THE ICE BOWL

You had to walk proud when you were with Lombardi, because he walked that way.

EMLEN TUNNELL

20 | *Make a Commitment to Excellence*

The year 1967 had been a tough one for the Green Bay Packers. The team finished the regular season with nine wins, four losses, and one tie—their worst record since missing the play-offs in '64. But they had managed to defeat the Los Angeles Rams in a Western Conference play-off game, 28–7. And on December 31, 1967, the Pack found themselves in the NFL title game going for a third straight championship—something that no team had ever before managed to achieve.

But there were two big obstacles standing in their way. First, they had to face the tough Dallas Cowboys—coached by Lombardi's friend and former colleague with the New York Giants, Tom Landry. Second, they had to overcome the worst weather conditions for a championship game in the history of the National Football League. A cold front had blown in overnight, and by seven o'clock that morning the temperature was sixteen degrees below zero. Inside a local hotel room, one of the Cowboys threw a cup of water on a window, and it instantly froze to ice.

"They're not going to play in this," said Willie Wood, whose car would not start. "It's just too damn cold."

Officials of the National Football League were seriously concerned about playing the game in such frigid temperatures. Jim Kensil and Mark Duncan, executive directors of the league, conferred with the Cowboy team doctor, who informed them that the only real danger was frostbite—and that could be averted by changing socks often and using common sense. Then they went over to the Packers' locker room and spoke with team doctor James Nellen, who was standing near Lombardi.

"I don't know what you guys are concerned about," interrupted Vince. "The weather's beautiful. The sun is shining. It's a great day!" Then he proceeded to show the NFL execs the control panel that heated the playing field. The previous off-season, Vince had spent $80,000 for the installation of an intricate grid of heating coils buried six inches below the turf. It was the latest in technology. It was Vince's baby. And boy, was he proud of it.

But something went wrong with the system that day—and Chuck Lane, the Packers' publicity director, had the unenviable task of informing Vince that the field had frozen over and, in some places, was as hard as a rock. "I never heard such a bellow in my life," recalled Lane.

"WHAT THE HELL ARE YOU TALKING ABOUT!?!" shrieked Lombardi.

The press would soon label the underground heating system "Lombardi's folly." But Vince was forced to put the failure behind him quickly. He had a job to do, a championship to win.

As big as the game was, Lombardi did not have much to say in the Packer locker room prior to his team taking the field. He had been building his guys up all week and, in truth, had already given them his pep talk. On Friday, he had said, "You're the type of ballplayers I want. You've got character. You've got heart. You've got guts. Okay, that's all. That's my pregame speech." And the players really didn't need to hear him say anything about the playing conditions. "You've got to be bigger than the weather to be a winner," he had told them many times in the past. "In any bitter contest, the winner will be whichever team wants it more."

By game time, the temperature was thirteen degrees below zero, with a minus-forty-six-degree windchill factor. People in the stands exhaled tens of thousands of puffs of vapored mist with every breath—and they were bundled up like Eskimos in the frozen Arctic. So were many of the Dallas Cowboys. With big warm gloves, stocking face masks, and hooded sweatshirts under their helmets, "they looked like earthmen on Mars," recalled Packer running back Chuck Mercein. In contrast, the Packers were dressed only as if it were just a bit colder than usual. And Lombardi had ordered that any player who handled the ball, including defensive players, could not wear gloves.

The Green Bay Packers, as a team and as individuals, could not know it at the time, but this particular game would be one of the most important and memorable events of their lives. Here, over the next three hours, under the most adverse playing conditions imaginable, all the values their coach had taught them, all the lessons he had drilled into them, would be brought to bear. Throughout the game, *Vince Lombardi's words* would pop into their minds, consciously and subconsciously. This would be *"the game where a man finds out what he's all about."* This would be the one moment in time when they would perform better than they ever thought they could perform, when they would be better than they ever thought they ever could be, and when they would become, as their coach often phrased it, *"men of character."*

Dallas took the opening kickoff from Green Bay but quickly had to punt the ball away. Tom Landry expected the Packers to stay on the ground, especially given the weather conditions. And that's exactly the way they started out—with three straight handoffs to running back Donny Anderson. But then Bart Starr, unexpectedly, took to the air and mounted a sixteen-play scoring drive that included eight running plays, eight passing plays, and two key Cowboy penalties. The drive culminated with an eight-yard touchdown pass to wide receiver Boyd Dowler.

Up in the television broadcast booth, Frank Gifford reached for a sip of his coffee. It had frozen solid. "The Packers lead the Cowboys 7–0," he said. "I think I'll take another bite of my coffee."

The remainder of the first quarter saw the two teams trade punts. But at the beginning of the second period, Lombardi put in two fresh running backs, Ben Wilson and Travis Williams. Clearly, Lombardi realized it was going to be a long, hard day—and the players were going to wear down fast. He had to keep their energy level up. (*"Fatigue makes cowards of us all."*)

Bart Starr employed the new men to help his team cross midfield and move into Cowboy territory. But then he surprised everybody by launching a forty-three-yard touchdown pass, again to Boyd Dowler. Now the Packers led 14–0. (*"Surprise should be based on deception and rapidity of maneuver."*)

On the very next series, Packer cornerback Herb Adderly intercepted a pass from Cowboy quarterback Don Meredith and returned it to the Dallas thirty-two-yard line. Green Bay was now threatening to turn the game into a rout. But the Cowboy defense rose to the occasion as George Andrie sacked Starr for a big loss, forcing the Packers to punt. However, the Dallas offense still could not mount a running attack against the Packers and had to kick once again. (*"Championship teams must stop the run."*)

Then, with five minutes left in the half, Willie Townes, Dallas defensive end, hit Starr in the backfield and forced a fumble. Andrie scooped up the loose ball and raced seven yards into the end zone for a touchdown. Now it was Green Bay 14, Dallas 7. Bart Starr didn't mince his words: "I should have tucked the ball away when I saw Townes coming, but he simply batted the thing loose." (*"Offer no excuses. Accept no excuses."*)

The two teams again traded punts. Only this time when the Cowboys kicked, Willie Wood fumbled the catch and Phil Clark of the Cowboys recovered on the Green Bay seventeen-yard-line. Like Starr, Wood, who was as sure-handed as they come, did not offer the weather and his cold hands as an excuse. "I blew the fair catch," he said simply. (*"Admit it when you make a mistake."*)

That turnover quickly resulted in a Danny Villaneuva twenty-one-yard field goal. Now Dallas trailed by only four points, 14–10, despite not having made a first down in the second quarter. And that's the way the half ended.

In the Packer locker room, Lombardi lamented the fact that they had utterly given away ten points and let the Cowboys back into the game. "The pendulum just swung Dallas's way," he said to Phil Bengtson. However, Vince did not lambaste his team. They needed the time to recover a little bit, to get warm, and to think about what had happened in the first half. So he let his assistant coaches talk a little bit about some key adjustments. (*"The conditions have to dictate what you say—or don't say."*)

Rather than being down on themselves, though, many of the players were amazed that Dallas had hung in there and actually come back from a two-touchdown deficit. "We had all gained great new respect for the Cowboys," recalled Forrest Gregg. (*"Respect your opponents."*)

When the two teams came out for the second half, the conditions appeared to have worsened. It seemed grayer, colder, a mess. "The wind, the cold, the conditions of the field—everything was deteriorating fast," said Gregg. "The [entire] field was hard as a rock. (*Adversity is the first path to truth.*")

Dallas kicked off to Green Bay to start the second half, and the Cowboy defense picked right up where it had left off. A key sack of Starr by Jethro Pugh forced the Packers to punt the ball away. Dallas then mounted a seven-minute drive behind the passing of Don Meredith and running of Dan Reeves. They drove the ball to the Green Bay eighteen before Lee Roy Caffey slammed into Meredith to force a fumble, which was recovered by Herb Adderly. The Packers had dodged a bullet.

After another Packer punt, Dallas was once more moving toward a score when Caffey again came out of nowhere to sack Don Meredith for a nine-yard loss. That forced a forty-seven-yard field goal attempt, which fell five yards short. Another Cowboy score had been averted by Green Bay because of the heroics of one man's inspired play. (*Each individual player has to do his own thinking and take responsibility for his own performance.*")

But the Cowboy defense did not let up. After the seventh sack of Bart Starr, the Packers, once again, had to kick the ball away—and the third quarter ended with the score still 14–10.

On the first play of the fourth quarter, halfback Dan Reeves took a pitchout from Don Meredith, scampered to his left, then stopped and threw a fifty-yard touchdown pass to receiver Lance Rentzel. The Cowboys had taken the lead, 17–14. And for the first time in the game, Green Bay found itself behind. But they refused to give up. (*The greatest glory is being knocked to your knees and rising again.*")

After trading punts, the Packers mounted a small drive but missed a forty-yard field goal attempt. As the clock began to tick away, Dallas took over on their own twenty. On the sidelines, Bob Lilly had been frantically massaging his quarterback's face—to no avail. In the huddle, Lance Rentzel had trouble understanding Don Meredith's play calls. "His cheeks were starting to freeze," said Rentzel.

The truth is that, by now, all players were feeling the long-term effects of the cold. They were moving slower and more gingerly. It was difficult keeping their balance. Fingers and toes were going numb. The ice on the field was now so jagged and razor-sharp that players ripped their jerseys on it when they fell. Running backs had difficulty holding onto the ball; receivers, catching it. Footing was terrible; turning was next to impossible. (*"Mental toughness, Spartanism, sacrifice, self-denial."*)

Still, the resilient Dallas Cowboys managed to gain two first downs and eat up several precious minutes off the clock. Finally, they were held in check by a proud Packer defense. (*"You were chosen to be a Green Bay Packer." "The Packers have pride."*)

So, with only four minutes and forty-five seconds left in the game, Green Bay's offense got the ball back on their own thirty-two-yard line. But they had gone nowhere in the entire second half up to that point, having managed only three first downs. Now they were up against the wall. This was it—do or die. For this final drive, they all had to execute *perfectly* under the worst of conditions. There would be no second chances—and everybody knew it.

It was all the more remarkable, then, that the Packer offensive unit felt tremendously confident. "We were gathered together on the side-lines," remembered Bob Skoronski, "and someone said, 'Well, we got it!'" (*"The man who is trained to his peak capacity will gain confidence."*)

As the offense ran onto the field, they passed the bruised and beaten-up defense trudging off. "Don't let me down," wheezed a battered Ray Nitschke, his voice almost gone from the cold, his feet frostbitten. "Don't let me down." (*"We have to pay a price for success."*)

In the huddle, Starr took a moment to glance around. "I just looked into the eyes of some of those guys," he said later. "Boyd Dowler, Jerry Kramer, Bob Skoronski, Forrest Gregg—we'd been working together for ten years, and it all came down to this drive. We all realized what had to be done and there was no point in putting it in words. We were ready. We were totally focused." (*"Success demands singleness of purpose."*)

"There was definitely a feel of urgency now in that huddle," said Chuck Mercein. "But there was calm, no panic, no desperation. I looked at some guys and nobody was looking downward; nobody's eyes were frantic. There was no feeling that we would not succeed." (*"The harder you work, the harder it is to surrender."*)

On the first play, Starr hit Donny Anderson with a pass that gained six yards. Then he handed the ball off to Mercein for seven more yards. Tackled next to the Packer bench, Mercein remembered that, "the guys were shaking their fists and yelling encouragement." (*"The success of the individual is completely subjected to the satisfaction that he receives in being part of the successful whole."*)

Then Starr completed a thirteen-yard pass to Boyd Dowler over the middle. Defensive end Cornell Green slammed Dowler to the ground and "bounced my head like a basketball on the ice." But Dowler got up, shook it off, and went back to the huddle. (*"You have to play with the small hurts. Hurt is in the mind."*)

Next the Packers ran the Lombardi Sweep. But Mercein missed his block and allowed Willie Townes to tackle Donny Anderson in the backfield for a nine-yard loss. "I felt absolutely terrible," remembered Mercein. "I went back to the huddle knowing that Chuck Mercein didn't do a good job on that block." "That was my responsibility," he told his teammates. (*"Offer no excuses. Accept no excuses."*)

Now faced with second down and nineteen yards to go, Donny Anderson told Starr he could get open for a pass out of the backfield if needed. The next two plays were passes drilled to Anderson for twelve and nine yards, respectively. First down, Packers. (*"Listen to the members of your team."*)

This time in the huddle, Chuck Mercein mentioned to his quarterback that the Cowboy defensive backs were dropping straight back rather than moving toward the sidelines. "If you need me, I'm open in the left flat," he said. Starr called the play and hit Mercein, who then dashed toward the clearing along the sidelines for nineteen yards—all the way down to the Dallas eleven-yard line. (*"Run to daylight, wherever it is."*)

"I was running at about eighty percent speed," recalled Mercein. "If I ran at a hundred percent I just wouldn't be able to keep my feet underneath me." (*"Think for yourself. Adjust on the fly."*)

Starr then turned to tackle Bob Skoronski and pointed out that Cowboy defensive end George Andrie was lining up a little off the line of scrimmage. (*"Pay attention to details."*) Could he block out Andrie, Bart wondered? "No problem," responded Skoronski. So Bart called a play designed to look like a Sweep. This would hopefully get Dallas All-Pro Bob Lilly to commit outside. Starr would then hand off to Mercein, who would cut inside.

"Fifty-four give, on one."

Starr moved right; Lilly committed; Mercein dashed up the middle for eight more yards. First down and goal on the Dallas three-yard line. (*"One must not hesitate to innovate."*)

Lombardi would later call this "one of the most inspired calls in championship history. It was set up to take advantage of the exceptional talent of Lilly. Lilly had been tearing us up all day. He was the heart of the Dallas defense." (*"That just shows you what a team can do when it takes advantage of the opponent's strength."*)

Starr next handed off to Donny Anderson, who took it straight up the middle for three more yards. The nose of the ball was placed just barely short of the goal line. As the clock continued to run, Bart called the same play. This should have done it. But Anderson slipped on the ice and lost a foot. (*"Make that second effort. Give it another try."*)

The Packers then called their final time-out with sixteen seconds left on the clock. It was third down and goal. As Starr headed over to the sidelines to confer with Lombardi, Forrest Gregg stopped him: "Tell Lombardi not to try that Sweep. We'd get tackled in the backfield for sure." (*"Teach people to think on the field to the degree that it becomes automatic."*)

With no time-outs left, a conservative approach might find the Packers next attempting a pass and, if it went incomplete, then kicking a field goal and sending the game into sudden death overtime. But the thought never entered Bart Starr's mind—nor the mind of any other Packer, for that matter. (*"When you get close to the goal line, your abandon is intensified." "Never be ready to settle for a tie." "The purpose of the game is to win." "There is no second place. Second place is meaningless." "If you could have won, you should have won."*)

Bart Starr, the Packers' leader on the field, the man who called the plays, said to Vince Lombardi: "Coach, if the line can get their footing, I can shuffle and lunge my way into the end zone." (*"Take the initiative."*)

And all Lombardi said was: "Then run it and let's get the hell out of here."

Back in the huddle, Starr called "thirty-one-wedge," which had become the lead play in that situation when Jerry Kramer recommended it during a film study session. "I noticed that Jethro Pugh was higher than Bob Lilly on a goal line charge," recalled Kramer. "So I said, 'Coach, if we need a wedge, we can wedge Pugh.'" Lombardi then ran the film back about three or four times and finally said, "That's right. Put in the wedge." (*"Study your opponent's past history. Determine strengths and weaknesses."*)

Thirty-one-wedge normally called for the fullback, Chuck Mercein, to carry the ball. But Starr did not want to risk a handoff or have Mercein slip on the ice (as Anderson had just done). "I'm running the sneak," Starr said in the huddle, "but you all block it like thirty-one-wedge." (*"Take charge."*) Mercein, perhaps because of the cold, only heard the words "thirty-one-wedge"—not that Starr was going to keep the ball.

The huddle broke and, as the Packers approached the line of scrimmage, Bob Lilly and Jethro Pugh were digging their heels into the frozen turf trying to get some traction. But as Pugh said, "My feet were too numb to scuff the ice."

All the players got set in their positions.

This was it. If the Packers did not make the touchdown, the clock would run out before they could kick a game-tying field goal. They were either going to win it or lose it on this, the last play of the game. (*"Winning isn't everything; it's the only thing." "The measure of each man is what he does in a specific situation." "If we fail now, we will fail in our other careers after football." "Run to win."*)

The front line stood like blocks of granite waiting for the snap count. Two years before, Lombardi had made them apologize in front of the entire team for a poor performance. There would be no apologies this time. Bob Skoronski, Gale Gillingham, Ken Bowman, Jerry Kramer, and Forrest Gregg were going to come off the line as one. (*"Together! Together! Not like a typewriter."*) They were going to be the greatest front line in football. (*"When those people walk out of the stands, I want that guy to turn to his wife and say, 'We just saw the greatest offensive linemen who ever played.'"*)

"Down, set, hut one." (*"People who work together will win."*)

Starr took the ball from Ken Bowman, then stepped forward and to the right. Jerry Kramer jumped a split second before the snap, but the referees did not notice. He hit Jethro Pugh low, Bowman hit him high, and both pushed Pugh backward. Forrest Gregg forced his man to the right—and Starr lunged for the opening. (*"Forget about being cautious. If you don't, you're licked before you start."*) In the same instant, Chuck Mercein bolted out of his stance like a big cat. Believing he was going to get the ball, he was "astonished when I plunged ahead to take the handoff and saw Bart carrying the ball instead!" As Starr crossed the goal line, Mercein was right behind him with his arms raised skyward—not to signal the touchdown but to show the referees that he had not pushed Starr into the end zone, which would have been a penalty. (*"The Green Bay Packers win because they do not make mistakes. Mister, we will not make mistakes."*)

With only a handful of seconds left on the clock, Green Bay had the lead, 21–17. And that's the way it ended. After a couple of desperation pass bombs by Don Meredith fell incomplete, the Packers were headed to Super Bowl II to meet the AFL champion Oakland Raiders.

After the game, Vince walked up to Donny Anderson. "He put his arm around me, hugged me, and said, 'Today, you became a man,'" recalled Anderson. "That game, in that last drive, was the best I ever played for the Green Bay Packers. All the hard work. All the discipline. All the good and all the bad were right there. You know, Lombardi just pushed you past every limit that you thought you had. That's what it's all about. . . ." (*"Battles are won primarily in the hearts of men."*)

As Lombardi, Anderson, and the rest of the Packers headed off the field, an element of pride could be detected in the way they walked. And watching at home on television, veteran Emlen Tunnell, long since retired, couldn't help but smile. "You had to walk proud when you were with Lombardi," remembered Tunnell, "because he walked that way."

Vince kept the press out of the locker room for the first few minutes. Alone with his players, he thanked them for their effort and told them how proud he was that they ran to win. Then he choked up and began to cry. "I can't talk anymore," he said as he knelt and led the team in prayer.

After the press was allowed in, a more composed Lombardi answered questions. About the final drive, he said: "It's not a question of what you tell [the players]. It's just a question of whether they realize, looking at the clock, that they only have a few minutes left. We didn't do anything differently. It took all of our poise, all of our experience."

To one reporter, talking about the last play, Lombardi said: "There was no question in my mind that we would run for the touchdown and that we would make it. . . . If you can't run the ball in there in a moment of crisis like that, then mister, you don't deserve to win. . . . Those types of decisions don't come from the mind; they come from the guts."

And to veteran television announcer Ray Scott he said: "We went for a touchdown instead of a field goal because I didn't want all those freezing people up in the stands to have to sit through a sudden death."

Scott never forgot the moment or the game. "I still say that final Packers drive was the greatest triumph of will over adversity that I have ever seen in any football game," he later marveled. "No pass was dropped, nobody fumbled, and you cannot imagine the conditions of their hands."

Also in the locker room after the game, Jerry Kramer was interviewed at length about his key block of Jethro Pugh. After a long pause, however, he looked dead into the lens of the camera and spoke about Lombardi. "Many things have been said about Coach, and he is not always understood by those who quote him," said Kramer to a national television audience. "The players understand. This is one beautiful man."

On the other side of the stadium, Tom Landry tried to console his dejected players. The Dallas Cowboys had made a great effort, played a mighty game. And he, perhaps more than anyone else, knew the real reason that the Packers had won the Ice Bowl.

"The discipline and conditioning programs they went through tend to develop character," Landry said. "And once you get character, you develop hope in all situations. Vince developed character in his players, character that a lot of them probably would never have had without [his] leadership. Therefore, they never were out of the game. They never felt like there wasn't some hope. And that is what carried them through to that third championship. That is what beat us."

Tom Landry's extraordinary insight was right on the mark. In essence, he credited the Packer win directly to the fact that Lombardi instilled character in his players.

But a leader must *have* character before he can instill it in others. And Vince Lombardi's reputation for personal character was of the highest order. His impeccable honesty and integrity was recognized by everyone who ever knew him. NFL commissioner Pete Rozelle, for instance, asserted that Vince was "a highly ethical person." Sports reporter Howard Cosell noted Lombardi's "total absence of hypocrisy," maintained that he was "dead honest," and contended that he had "absolutely no malice." And Fr. David Rondou, Lombardi's priest, said: "What guided Vince most was fair play. He coached and he did everything with that in mind—a recognition of the other man. You could almost use the word *justice*. If it was right, if it was just, well then, he'd go ahead with it. If it was wrong or unjust, he couldn't do it."

Lombardi was the same person whether he was on the practice field with his team, or in the boardroom with executives, or at home with his family. He demanded more of himself than he did of anyone else, and he practiced *exactly* what he preached: "A good leader must first discipline himself before he can discipline others. A man should not ask others to do things he would not have asked himself to do at one time or another in his life."

"If we would create something," said Vince Lombardi, "we must be something."

He was a man who took himself very seriously. A perfectionist by nature, Vince had an inner strength that was sustained largely by his spirituality. "He never did anything without prayer," said his daughter, Susan. Of his team's pregame prayers, Vince noted that "we don't pray to win; we pray to play the best we can and to keep us free from injury. And the prayer we say after the game is one of thanksgiving."

But perhaps the most enduring element of Vince Lombardi's character is that he constantly sought to raise the bar. His leadership was not simply based on winning football games or making a profit but on a much more noble principle. "The value of all our daily efforts is greater and more enduring if they create in each one of us a person who grows and understands and really lives," he said. "Of one who prevails for a larger and more meaningful victory. Not only now, but in time and, hopefully, in eternity."

To a man, the athletes who played for him recognized this higher standard, this deeper sentiment, almost immediately. "Winning to Lombardi was neither everything nor the only thing," noted Bart Starr. "He was more interested in seeing us make the effort to be our best. If we did, he knew that winning would usually take care of itself."

So there it is. Vince Lombardi taught his players to do things right, not just once in a while but all the time. More than that, though, he attempted to create in them a will, a burning desire, to always do the right thing.

"Listen, I know you can't be perfect," he'd say to his players like a father speaking to his sons. "No one is perfect. But boys, making the effort to be perfect, trying as hard as you can, is what life is all about. If you'll not settle for anything less than the best, you will be amazed at what you can do with your lives. You'll be amazed at how much you can rise in the world. . . . The quality of a man's life has got to be a full measure of that man's personal commitment to excellence and victory, regardless of what field he may be in."

Triumph in the Ice Bowl was not the ultimate victory for Vince Lombardi—nor was the success in Super Bowl II that secured a third straight national championship. "The ultimate victory can never be won," he maintained. "Yet it must be pursued with all one's might."

Ultimate success can only be achieved in a person's heart. And Vince Lombardi's was the heart of a very good and decent man.

"After the cheers have died down and the stadium is empty," said Lombardi, "after the headlines have been written and after you are back in the quiet of your own room and the championship ring has been placed on the dresser and all the pomp and fanfare have faded, the enduring thing that is left is the dedication to doing with our lives the very best we can to make the world a better place in which to live."

Lombardi Principles

- A leader must *have* character before he can instill it in others.
- If we would create something, we must be something.
- Whatever it may be, a leader has got to get across to his team that feeling of truth, that feeling of honesty, that feeling of selflessness. Do you see?
- Be the same person whether you are on the practice field with your team, in the boardroom with executives, or at home with your family.
- To stay a leader, you must be prepared to adhere to your principles if you are certain, in your own conscience, that you are doing right.
- Do your job the way you're convinced is right for you. The rest will follow or it won't work.
- Unless a man believes in himself and makes a total commitment to his career and puts everything he has into it—his mind, his body, and his heart—what's life worth to him?
- Do not ask others to do something that you yourself would not do.
- Constantly seek to raise the bar. People will immediately recognize your higher standard.
- Teach your team to do things right all the time. Create in them a will to do the right thing.
- Make the effort to be perfect; that is what life is all about.
- The quality of a man's life has got to be a full measure of that man's personal commitment to excellence.
- Do with your life the very best you can to make the world a better place in which to live.

Super Bowl II was played on January 14, 1968, before 75,000 fans in warm Miami, Florida. For the Green Bay Packers, it was both anticlimactic and a picnic compared to what they had been through two weeks earlier in the Ice Bowl.

Their opponent was the AFL champion Oakland Raiders, led by quarterback Daryle Lamonica and aging veteran George Blanda, still performing the kicking chores. Viewed as an offensive powerhouse, Oakland had annihilated the Houston Oilers 40–7 in the AFL title game.

The Raiders would not fare so well against Green Bay this day, however. Three field goals by Don Chandler and a sixty-eight-yard touchdown pass from Bart Starr to Boyd Dowler offset a lone Raider touchdown in the first half—and the Packers took a 16–7 lead into the locker room at the break.

Vince Lombardi planned to retire to the Packer head office at the conclusion of the season, and word had leaked out to the players that this would be Lombardi's last game. Vince himself unintentionally dropped a hint at the team's final film session the previous Friday. "Okay, boys," he had said, "this may be the last time we'll be together, so . . . uh . . ." He was unable to complete the sentence. Overcome by emotion, Vince simply turned to face the movie screen and sat down. Lights out; roll the film.

Most of the veterans knew what that meant, and they were determined to have him go out a winner. At halftime, Jerry Kramer pulled the team together when Vince was out of the room. "Let's play these last thirty minutes for the old man," Kramer said.

The second half was all Green Bay. The Packers stormed out and scored seventeen unanswered points. Their ball-control offense engineered a touchdown and a field goal—and the defense held Oakland to only one late-in-the-game score. When Herb Adderly intercepted a Lamonica pass in the fourth quarter and ran it back sixty yards for a touchdown, it was over. The final score was: Green Bay 33, Oakland 14.

When time ran out, Forrest Gregg and Jerry Kramer lifted their coach high in triumph and carried him off on their shoulders.

"Now, this is the way to leave a football field!" shouted Lombardi.

I jog in the morning, and there are days when I wake up and I don't feel like getting up and crawling into the office. Then I think, What would Lombardi do? *I get up and out of bed, and I throw on my sweats and I jog.*

WILLIE DAVIS

Epilogue

A month after Super Bowl II, Lombardi turned over the Packer head coaching job to Phil Bengtson and retired to the front office, maintaining his position as general manager. At the press conference, he cited "the nature [and growth] of the business" as a reason for his decision, but Vince was also physically exhausted and mentally spent. Over the previous year, he had experienced chest pains, fainting spells, painful arthritis in his hip, a bad stomach, and a variety of intestinal problems. As several people close to him noticed, "he just looked tired all the time."

But taking time off from coaching might have been the worst thing Lombardi could have done—at least for his mental health. He became fidgety, nervous, restless. Never really interested in business matters all that much, he avoided the day-to-day paperwork routine and, soon, didn't know what to do with himself. But he also refused to criticize or interfere with Bengtson's handling of the team. So the only thing left for Lombardi to do was sit back and watch. And predictably, his stomach churned even more as he wallowed in inactivity and frustration.

"It's murder," he told a friend after only a few months. "I never knew I'd miss it this much. . . . I made a big mistake."

It turned out that the Packers missed Vince as much as he missed them. The players appeared less inspired and focused as their record progressed toward a season-ending 6-7-1. And they seemed concerned about the forlorn look in Lombardi's eyes whenever he happened to drop by and wander the sidelines during a practice session. "Hey, Coach," Henry Jordan once yelled from the field, "do you want to chew us out for old times' sake?"

A year's worth of inactivity was too much for Lombardi to endure. So he began fielding coaching offers from other teams. Finally, on February 1, 1969, Vince accepted the proposal of Edward Bennett Williams to make him head coach, general manager, and part-owner of the Washington Redskins.

With a 6–9 won-loss record in '68, the Redskins had suffered their fourteenth losing season in a row. But in 1969, under Vince Lombardi's leadership, they finished 7-5-2. The entire demeanor and feeling of the team had turned around in just one year. And everybody—fans, staff, and players—was looking forward with excitement and anticipation to the upcoming 1970 season. "We all had hope now," recalled Sonny Jurgensen, who, in 1969, had shed his trademark potbelly for Lombardi and enjoyed the best year of his career.

In the off-season, Vince pulled his new field leader aside and gave him an inkling of what to expect for the '70 season. "My year out of football really softened me up," he told Jurgensen. "It really did. I was just too easy on you guys last year. I let you all get away with too much. That's why we didn't win more games. This year, I'm gonna be tougher than I've ever been. And I'm gonna be tougher on you than anybody else."

But it was not to be.

During an early training camp in June, Vince became light-headed and nearly collapsed. "I'm so damn tired I cannot stand up," he told an assistant coach. Within two weeks, Lombardi was admitted to Georgetown University Hospital—the first time in his entire life he had ever been a hospital patient. A sigmoidoscopy and biopsy disclosed cancer of the colon. That led to an immediate operation in which a two-foot section of Lombardi's large intestine was removed. He was sent home to recuperate, but one month later he began having more abdominal pain. Immediately readmitted to the hospital, Vince underwent additional tests and exploratory surgery, which revealed not only another tumor in the colon but also that the cancer had spread to his liver and lymph nodes. The physicians were shocked. This was no ordinary cancer. It was vicious. "I've done thousands of cases of colon cancer," said Dr. Robert Coffey, "and I've never seen one this virulent." He informed the Lombardis that there was no hope—the prognosis was terminal. All they could do now, he said, was implement chemotherapy and radiation treatment—and pray.

But Vince Lombardi was a coach. He had never lost a game, remember. Sometimes the clock runs out too early, but if you play long enough, you'll win. So for most of the two months Vince was in the hospital, he was positive and encouraging. "I'm gonna beat this thing," he assured his wife and family. "Don't worry about me," he told his friends. "I'll lick this." He also began instructing the doctors, nurses, and orderlies on how they could run things more efficiently. Vince was particularly tough on one young intern who tended to talk to the nurses while ignoring his patients. "What's going on around here?" Lombardi would constantly ask. "[He] just raised hell with everybody," remembered one staff member.

But after a few short weeks, the doctors, nurses, and orderlies began visiting Vince in their off-duty hours. And that young intern could no longer be seen loitering in the halls chatting with the pretty nurses. "Where is he?" someone on the staff would ask. "He's in talking to a patient," the answer invariably came back.

As word of the seriousness of Lombardi's condition filtered out, people began streaming to his bedside. In came past and present staff members, assistant coaches, owners, colleagues, and close friends. And one by one, sometimes two by two, "they" came—Lombardi's players, his sons, his "boys." Frank Gifford, Paul Hornung, Bart Starr and Zeke Bratkowski, Fuzzy Thurston and Bob Skoronski, Willie Wood, Forrest Gregg, Jerry Kramer, Chuck Mercein, and Sonny Jurgensen, to name just a few. Many stayed only a few minutes, because they couldn't speak, couldn't find the words to say what was in their hearts.

Bill Curry managed to get a few words out. "Coach," he said. "I just want you to know that honestly, without bitterness, looking at the time I spent with you, you've really meant a lot to my life."

Vince shook Curry's hand in response. "Bill, you can mean a lot to my life right now if you can pray."

"With that, I couldn't speak anymore," remembered Curry. "I just nodded."

Willie Davis hopped a plane from San Diego. When he walked into the hospital room, the coach greeted him with tears in his eyes. "Willie," said Vince after a few minutes, "you're one of the finest young men I've ever . . ." Lombardi began to cry and could not go on. Davis left the room after a moment, but stood crying himself in the hospital corridor for a half hour, his head resting against the wall.

As time wore on, Vince lost more and more weight, became more and more tired. He prayed with his priest. If he had to do anything over again, he said, he'd "pray for more patience and understanding." "I'm not afraid to meet my God now," he told his old friend Fr. Timothy Moore. 'But what I do regret is that there is so damn much left to be done here on Earth."

By the end of August, he was fading in and out of a deep sleep. Mostly, though, he slept. On August 31, the Lombardis' thirtieth wedding anniversary, Vince opened his eyes briefly and said to Marie: "Happy Anniversary, Rie. Remember, I love you."

Four days later, time finally ran out. At 7:20 A.M. on the third of September 1970, Vince Lombardi died. He was fifty-seven years old.

Three thousand people attended the funeral mass at St. Patrick's Cathedral in New York. Afterward a procession of forty limousines took a slow one-hour journey to Mount Olivet Cemetery near Red Bank, New Jersey. All along the way, in every small hamlet and town, people gathered to pay their respects in silence as the motorcade passed. Before the body was laid to rest, Vince's father, Harry, looked over at Jerry Kramer, smiled, and said softly, "He loved you boys. He loved you boys."

In January 1959, everybody in Green Bay, Wisconsin, was asking the same question: "Who in hell is Vincent Lombardi?" In most people's minds, he was an unknown "old man" seemingly unable to handle the head coaching job of their beloved Packers. But at the time of his death, a little more than a decade later, he was one of the most famous men in the country.

Vince Lombardi turned out to have made all the difference in the world—and his performance is now the standard by which all others in his profession are judged. In nine years at Green Bay, he accumulated six Western Conference championships, five NFL championships, and two Super Bowl victories. He was named Coach of the Year four times, won nine of ten postseason games, and had an overall .758 winning percentage. He never had a losing season or even a .500 season. He always had winning seasons. In 1971, on the heels of Lombardi's posthumous induction into the NFL Hall of Fame, Commissioner Pete Rozelle renamed the silver Super Bowl award the Vince Lombardi Trophy. The second person it was handed to with the new name was, of all people, Tom Landry—for the Dallas Cowboys' victory in Super Bowl VI. Forrest Gregg and Herb Adderly, who had been traded from the Packers to the Cowboys the previous year, were also on that championship team.

Lombardi's impact on his profession was profound. But he had an even greater influence on the people with whom he came into contact over the course of his life. "He wasn't all things to all people, but he was someone to everyone," said Lionel Aldridge. "He's the greatest coach I ever played under," said Paul Hornung. "I would have gone through a wall for that guy." And Phil Bengtson declared that "if I were lost in the middle of nowhere with only one dime for the pay telephone and needed a doctor, a lawyer, a priest, and a friend, I'd call Vince Lombardi."

Most players immediately realized what they had lost—and despaired of ever seeing the likes of it again. "All the things a man searches for all his life I found in Coach Lombardi," said the Redskins' Jerry Smith. "All the time I spend around football, I'm always fishing around looking to find someone like him," said Emlen Tunnell. "But I never have. And I know I never will."

In the many tributes and recollections since Lombardi's death, two words—*love* and *father*—have often been repeated by the players. "I loved Vince," said Frank Gifford. "[He was] the biggest influence of my life, even more than my own father." "If you could select your own father," said Sam Huff, "you would want him to be like Vince." "I think of Lombardi every day," Herb Adderly told Jerry Kramer. "I love my father, who is also deceased, but I don't think about my father every day."

These were grown men speaking about loving another man as much as they loved their own dads. That certainly indicates something more than simply a coach/player type of relationship. To some, Lombardi was a father teaching his sons:

Bill Curry: "He was making me grow up when I didn't want to. He was thinking of me.

Ray Nitschke: "He helped to turn me around as a person."

Bart Starr: "More than anything else, he wanted us to be great men after we'd left football."

To others, he was a benefactor who gave them a helping hand up the ladder of life:

Paul Hornung: "Without him, I don't know where I'd be today."

Gary Knafelc: "He changed my life entirely."

Bart Starr: "I owe my life to that man."

To still others, he was a motivator, philosopher, and teacher:

Sam Huff: "He got more out of me than I ever thought I could give."

Vince Promuto: "If he taught us anything, he taught every one of us to respect ourselves."

Chris Hanburger: "He was a teacher about life itself. A lot of my standards in life, I developed from him."

And to all, he left an indelible impression that would stick with them the rest of their lives:

Jerry Kramer: "I've got an edge, because whenever I'm tempted to screw off, to cut corners, I hear that raspy voice saying: 'This is the right way to do it. Which way are you going to do it, mister?'"

Willie Davis: "I jog in the morning, and there are days when I wake up and I don't feel like getting up and crawling into the office. Then I think, *What would Lombardi do?* I get up and out of bed, and I throw on my sweats and I jog."

Bill Curry: "To this day, anytime I'm in a bind with a difficult problem to overcome, without exception, I always think of him. Always! I think of him telling me, 'Son, the only thing you can do is to get off your ass and stop feeling sorry for yourself and overcome the pain and *do it!* Work out your method. Work out your system, and execute it. And don't tell me about a sprained ankle, and don't tell me that somebody's not being fair to you. I don't want to hear *any* of that. Do it!' "

Perhaps, more than anything else, Vince Lombardi was the players' idea of what a great leader should be. And who better to judge leadership qualities in a person than the people being led? "When I think of Lombardi," said Marv Fleming, "I think of Martin Luther King. I think of Gandhi. I think of great people who led the way for freedom and the right way of life." Bart Starr concurred: "To me, Coach Lombardi would gather the masses behind him, and people would want to identify with someone like that."

"Leadership rests not only upon ability," said Lombardi, "but upon commitment and upon loyalty and upon pride and upon followers. . . . Leadership is not just one quality, but rather a blend of many qualities; and while no one individual possesses all the needed talents to go into leadership, each man can develop a combination to make him a leader."

To a great degree, that's exactly what Lombardi did. He was able to combine a caring and compassionate nature with an enviable ability to get things done. Lombardi had heart—and he had goals that went beyond the game of football. Moreover, he was able to successfully achieve those goals by employing a strong measure of ethics and morality. "Your moral integrity is the most priceless thing you possess," he lectured his players. "With Lombardi," remembered Sonny Jurgensen, "cheating was out."

Vince Lombardi's principles, his style, and the way he lived his life can be employed as a sterling model for effective leadership in any organization—football, business, and beyond. His insight into the problems that continuously face a struggling world are still appropriate today. And his words, even though spoken more than thirty years ago, can serve to guide any society searching for a better way.

"In a large sense, we are engaged right now in a struggle that is far more fiercely contested than any game," he said. "It is a struggle for the hearts, for the minds, and for the souls of all of us, and it is a game in which there are no spectators, only players. . . . The test of this century will be whether man mistakes the growth of wealth and power with the growth of spirit and character . . . [Our country needs] people who will keep their heads in emergencies; in other words, leaders who will meet the intricate problems with wisdom and courage."

Every Thursday morning, Vince Lombardi would trot onto the practice field to meet his players. As everyone assembled for calisthenics, he would ask one question. A question that only they could answer.

"Who leads today?" he would ask.

Who leads today?

All right! That's all.
VINCE LOMBARDI

ACKNOWLEDGMENTS

I'd like to thank Grant Teaff and Walter Abercrombie of the American Football Coaches Association for their support and technical assistance during the research and writing of this project. Rick Wolff came up with the original idea for the book—for which I'm very grateful. My good friend David Johnson provided invaluable support and technical assistance that helped me understand the finer points of both Vince Lombardi and the game of football. I also thank Anne Marie Rozelle Bratton and Vince Lombardi, Jr., for previewing the early manuscript and lending their support and endorsement. Marc Resnick, a senior editor at St. Martin's Press, has made a great contribution to the text and has been a pleasure to work with. As usual, my friend and agent Bob Barnett deserves tremendous credit for pulling everything together and making it all happen. Finally, I thank all the people with whom I spoke who knew Vince Lombardi and shared their stories with me. Most especially, I wish to acknowledge the assistance of Coach Tom Landry, whose personal insights into Vince Lombardi were invaluable. Coach Landry also touched me deeply. He was a great man.

BIBLIOGRAPHY

Bengtson, Phil, with Todd Hunt. *Packer Dynasty*. Garden City, NY: Doubleday, 1969.

Blaik, Earl H., with Tim Cohane. *You Have to Pay the Price: The Red Blaik Story*. New York: Holt, Rinehart and Winston, 1960.

Briggs, Jennifer, ed. *Strive to Excel: The Will and Wisdom of Vince Lombardi*. Nashville, TN: Rutledge Hill Press, 1997.

Brown, Larry, with William Gildea. *I'll Always Get Up*. New York: Simon and Schuster, 1973.

Bynum, Mike, ed. *Vince Lombardi: Memories of a Special Time*. October Football, 1988.

Cox, Ignatius W. *Liberty: Its Use and Abuse: Principles of Ethics, Basic and Applied*. New York: Fordham University Press, 1936.

Dowling, Tom. *Coach: A Season with Lombardi*. New York: Norton, 1970.

Eskenazi, Gerald. *There Were Giants in Those Days*. New York: Simon and Schuster, 1987.

Etter, Les. *Vince Lombardi: Football Legend*. Champaign, IL: Garrard, 1975.

Flynn, George L. *Vince Lombardi on Football*. New York: New York Graphic Society, 1973.

———. *The Vince Lombardi Scrapbook*. New York: Grossett and Dunlap, 1976.

George, Gary, ed. *Winning Is a Habit*. New York: HarperCollins, 1997.

Gifford, Frank. *The Golden Year, 1956*. Englewood Cliffs, NJ: William N. Wallace/Prentice-Hall, 1969.

———. *The Whole Ten Yards*. New York: Ballantine, 1994.

Gruver, Ed. *Ice Bowl: The Cold Truth About Football's Most Unforgettable Game*. Ithaca, New York: McBooks, 1998.

Hornung, Paul, with Al Silverman. *Football and the Single Man*. New York: Doubleday, 1965.

Klein, Dave. *The Vince Lombardi Story*. New York: Lion Books, 1971.

Kramer, Jerry, with Dick Schaap. *Instant Replay*. New York: World, 1968.

————, ed. *Lombardi: Winning Is the Only Thing*. New York: World, 1970.

Landry, Tom, with Gregg Lewis. *Tom Landry: An Autobiography*. New York: HarperCollins, 1990.

Lombardi, Vince. *Second Effort*. (Video.) Chicago: Dartnell, 1968.

Lombardi, Vince, with W. C. Heinz. *Run to Daylight*. Englewood Cliffs, NJ: Prentice-Hall, 1963.

Lombardi, Vince, Jr. *Baby Steps to Success*. Lancaster, PA: Starburst, 1997.

Madden, John, with Dave Anderson. *All Madden: Hey, I'm Talking Pro Football*. New York: HarperCollins, 1996.

Mariniss, David. *When Pride Still Mattered: A Life of Vince Lombardi*. New York: Simon and Schuster, 1999.

May, Julian. *Vince Lombardi: The Immortal Coach*. Mankato, MN: Crestwood House, 1975.

Nitschke, Ray, with Robert W. Wells. *Mean on Sunday*. Garden City, NY: Doubleday, 1973.

O'Brien, Michael. *Vince: A Personal Biography of Vince Lombardi*. New York: Quill/William Morrow, 1987.

Paterno, Joe, with Bernard Asbell. *Paterno by the Book*. New York: Random House, 1989.

Plimpton, George. *One More July. A Football Dialogue with Bill Curry*. New York: Harper and Row, 1977.

Schoor, Gene. *Football's Greatest Coach: Vince Lombardi*. Garden City, NY: Doubleday, 1974.

Shropshire, Mike. *The Ice Bowl*. New York: Donald I. Fine, 1997.

Siegener, Ray, ed. *The Vince Lombardi Pro Football Guide '70*. Nashville, TN: Aurora, 1970.

Starr, Bart, and John Wiebusch. *A Perspective on Victory*. Chicago: Follett, 1972.

Starr, Bart, with Murray Oldeman. *Starr: My Life in Football*. New York: Morrow, 1987.

Wells, Robert. W. *Vince Lombardi: His Life and Times*. Madison, WI: Prairie Oak Press, 1997.

Whittingham, Richard. *Giants in Their Own Words*. Chicago: Contemporary Books, 1992.

Wiebusch, John, ed. *Lombardi*. Chicago: Triumph Books, 1997.

Wukovits, John. *Vince Lombardi*. Philadelphia: Chelsea House, 1997.

INDEX

Adderly, Herb, 20, 28
  on Lombardi, 178
  1967 NFL championship game, 163,
    164
  Super Bowl II, 173
  Super Bowl VI, 178
Aldridge, Lionel, 105, 107, 116, 132,
  158, 178
Anderson, Donny
  1967 NFL championship game, 162,
    165, 166, 167, 169
Andrie, George
  1967 NFL championship game, 163,
    166
Associated Press, 129
Austin, Bill, 23, 87, 139, 146, 153–54

ball control, 34–35
Baltimore Colts, 6, 33, 73–74, 129
  1958 NFL championship game,
    121–22
Bankstone, Willie, 105
Bednarik, Chuck, 44
Bengtson, Phil, 18–19, 25, 40, 78, 100,
  135–36, 163, 174
  on Lombardi as coach, 178
Blaik, Earl "Red," 4–5, 14, 15, 39, 49,
  90–91, 123
  on the will to win, 116, 118
Blanda, George, 173
Bowman, Ken, 138, 141, 168
Bratkowski, Zeke, 69, 113
  visiting Lombardi in the hospital, 176
Brooklyn Eagles football team, 3
Brooklyn Prep football team, 72–73
Brown, Allen, 75–76
Brown, Jim, 34
Brown, Larry, 29, 59, 113
Brown, Paul, 14, 130
Brown, Tom, 76

Brunet, Bob, 58–59, 139
building trust, Lombardi on, 45

Caffey, Lee Roy, 104, 118, 164
Canadeo, Tony, 51
Carpenter, Lew, 9, 20, 23
CBS, 7
Chandler, Don, 23, 25, 58, 173
change, Lombardi on, 37, 41
character, Lombardi on, 127
Chicago Bears, 6, 9, 129
Churchill, Winston, 132
Clark, Phil, 163
Cleveland Browns, 34, 129
Cochran, John, 19, 156
Coffey, Robert, 176
commitment to excellence, Lombardi
  on, 160
Conerly, Charlie, 85, 106
Cosell, Howard, 170
creativity, 37–42
  Lombardi on, 37
Crowley, Jim, 2, 73, 91
Currie, Dan, 20, 59
Curry, Bill, 87
  on the conditioning routine, 99
  on film analysis and recap, 94
  on Lombardi, 178, 179–80
  on Lombardi and the dog, 88
  on Lombardi as an influence, 107
  on Lombardi and winning, 122
  and Lombardi's temper, 103, 116,
    139
  visiting Lombardi in the hospital, 176

Dallas Cowboys, 6, 33, 118
  1966 NFL championship game, 125
  1967 NFL championship game,
    160–68
  Super Bowl VI, 178

Davis, Willie, 75
  Lombardi on, 56
  on Lombardi, 179
  and Lombardi as coach, 117
  and Lombardi as an inspiration, 30,
    74, 76, 157
  and Lombardi on race, 64, 65
  on Lombardi and simplicity, 69
  on Lombardi's delegating decisions,
    111
  on Lombardi's kindness, 150
  and Lombardi's motivational impact,
    117, 119
  and Lombardi's sensitivity, 144
  on Lombardi's will to win, 119
  on losing, 131
  as player, 19, 21
  on Super Bowl II, 173–74
  visiting Lombardi in the hospital, 177
Dawson, Len, 125, 125–26
defeat, Lombardi on, 129, 131
Detroit Lions, 49, 74, 133, 146
discipline, 98–107, 170
"Do-Dad" blocking, 39–40
Dowler, Boyd, 55, 58, 106, 112, 120,
    173
  1967 NFL championship game, 162,
    163, 165, 165–66
drilling the team, Lombardi on, 81
Duncan, Mark, 86, 161

excellence, commitment to, 160–71
  Lombardi on, 160
expertise, 25–30

family, 144–51
  Lombardi and, 149–50
  Lombardi on, 144, 147–48, 150–51
Fears, Tom, 19, 150
Ferguson, Howie, 84–85
film and video analysis, 39, 93–94
Fischer, Pat, 52, 70, 77
Fleming, Marv, 75, 180
Fordham Rams, 32
Fordham University, 2, 3, 4, 38, 50
Forrester, Bill, 20, 120, 150

game plan, developing a, 32–35
  Lombardi on, 32
Gifford, Frank
  as broadcaster, 162
  on Lombardi as coach, 58, 92, 132,
    178
  on Lombardi as example, 51
  on Lombardi's enthusiasm, 49
  on Lombardi's temper, 140
  as player, 16, 54, 85, 109–10, 110
  visiting Lombardi in the hospital, 176
Gillingham, Gale, 168
Green, Cornell, 166
Green Bay (WI)
  and racism, 63–64
Green Bay Packers, 1, 6–7, 9, 13–14, 44
  and the call-up of reserves, 120
  championships, 7, 44, 49, 74, 80,
    129–30, 156, 160
  honors assembly, 95
  1962 NFL championship game, 123
  1966 NFL championship game, 125
  1967 NFL championship game,
    160–68
  and racism, 63–64
  Super Bowl I, 33, 125–26
  Super Bowl II, 7, 49–50, 168, 171,
    173–74
  See also Lombardi, Vincent (career:
    leadership process)
Gregg, Forrest, 22
  on film analysis and recap, 93–94
  Lombardi on, 16, 55
  on Lombardi and teamwork, 47
  on Lombardi as coach, 52
  on Lombardi's opening remarks, 84
  and Lombardi's motivational impact,
    117
  1967 NFL championship game,
    163–64, 165, 167, 168
  on Super Bowl I, 125
  Super Bowl II, 173
  Super Bowl VI, 178
  visiting Lombardi in the hospital, 176
Gremminger, Hank, 20
Gros, Earl, 150

Haas, Robert, 96
Halas, George, 14, 38
Hall of Fame (National Football
    League), 7
Hanburger, Chris, on Lombardi, 179
Hanner, Dave (Hawg), 20
heart power, 144–51
  Lombardi on, 144, 147–48, 150–51
Hecker, Norb, 77–78
  as coach, 18, 30, 135–36
  on working for Lombardi, 25
Heinz, Bill, 33, 119
Heinz, W. C., 55
honors assembly, 95

Hornung, Paul, 48
 and the Berlin Crisis call-up, 120
 breaking curfew, 101–2
 Lombardi on, 16, 56
 on Lombardi, 179
 on Lombardi as coach, 178
 on Lombardi as teacher, 91–92
 on Lombardi's game preparation, 33,
  35
 and Lombardi's motivating, 88, 104
 Lombardi's putting on draft list,
  144–45
 as player, 9, 20, 21, 54, 80, 110
 playing with injuries, 106
 visiting Lombardi in the hospital, 176
Howell, Jim Lee, 6, 139
Howton, Billy, 21
Huff, Sam, 23, 80, 132, 157, 178

imagination, 37–42
Iman, Ken, 104
individuals, treating people as, 54–60
 Lombardi on, 54
innovation, 37–42
 Lombardi on, 37
inspiration, 72–78
 Lombardi on, 72

Jeter, Bob, 150
Jordan, Henry, 175
 Lombardi on, 56
 on Lombardi's delegating decisions,
  111, 112
 on Lombardi's force of will, 88
 on Lombardi's kindness, 150
 on Lombardi's physical conditioning,
  99, 100, 106–7
 on Lombardi's setting an example, 51
 as player, 19, 21
Jordan, Olive (wife), 151
Jordan, Suzanne (daughter), 151
Jurgensen, Sonny, 175
 as a player, 57–58, 83
 on Lombardi and cheating, 180
 on Lombardi as a coach, 74, 92
 on Lombardi as an influence, 107
 visiting Lombardi in the hospital, 176

Kane, Harry, 2, 91
Kansas City Chiefs, 33–34
 Super Bowl I, 125–26
Karras, Alex, 146
keeping things simple, Lombardi on, 67
Kennedy, John F., 120

Kensil, Jim, 161
Knaflec, Gary, 88, 95, 96, 101
 on Lombardi, 179
knowledge, 25–30
Kramer, Jerry, 110, 118
 on film analysis and recap, 92–93, 94
 Lombardi on, 56
 on Lombardi, 179
 on Lombardi as coach, 1, 7, 25, 37,
  74, 141, 154, 157
 on Lombardi as teacher, 96
 on Lombardi and team injuries, 105
 on Lombardi's leadership, 87
 and Lombardi's motivation, 76, 77,
  145
 on Lombardi's rules, 102
 and Lombardi's sensitivity, 144–45
 and Lombardi's temper, 138
 1967 NFL championship game, 165,
  167, 168, 169
 playing with injuries, 106
 on running to daylight, 100
 Super Bowl II, 173
 visiting Lombardi in the hospital, 176,
  177
 on workouts, 100
Krueger, Ockie, 69, 142

Lambeau, Earl "Curly," 13
Lambeau Field (Green Bay, WI), 39
Lamonica, Daryle, 173
Landry, Tom, 6, 26, 54, 119, 122, 160
 on Lombardi's leadership, 160
 1967 NFL championship game, 160,
  162, 170
 and the Vince Lombardi Trophy, 178
Lane, Chuck, 161
Larson, Greg, 80
Lawlor, Jim, 64–65, 133
lead, the courage to, 129–33
 Lombardi on, 83
Leahy, Frank, 2–3, 38, 91
learning, 90–96
 Lombardi on, 90
Lilly, Bob
 1967 NFL championship game, 164,
  166–67, 167, 168
Lincoln, Abraham, 132
Lombardi, Harry (father), 1, 177
Lombardi, Marie Planitz (wife), 4, 15
 as a football widow, 158
 on Lombardi as teacher, 96
 on Lombardi setting an example, 52
 and Lombardi's death, 177

Lombardi, Marie Planitz (*continued*)
  on Lombardi's color blindness, 65
  on Lombardi's personality, 141–42, 153, 155
  and Lombardi's rules, 102
  on Lombardi's simplicity, 70
  on Lombardi's temper, 137, 141–42
Lombardi, Matilda (mother), 1
Lombardi, Susan (daughter), 142, 153, 170
Lombardi, Vincent
  Catholicism of, 1, 139–40, 148, 155, 170–71
  charitable associations, 148–49
  childhood and education, 1–3, 32, 119–20
  death and funeral, 175–77
  mentors, 2–3, 4–5, 90–91, 118, 123
  sports, early participation in, 2–4, 32, 50
Lombardi, Vincent (appearance, personality, and temperament), 3, 7, 132
  confrontation, creating, 104–5
  enthusiasm and passion, 49, 69, 80
  as an example, 51–52
  giving credit and taking responsibility, 49–50
  honesty and sincerity, 48–49, 65, 69, 131–32
  informality, 50–51
  injuries, having plays play through, 105–6
  courage and loyalty, 50, 132
  motivational impact, 116–19
  and prejudice, 62–66
  principles, 17, 24, 31, 36, 43, 53, 61, 66, 71, 79, 89, 97, 108, 115, 124, 134, 143, 152, 159, 172, 180–81
  relationships and distance, 58, 87–88
  self-control, 135–43
  temper, 58–59, 67–68, 75–76, 77–78, 103–4, 116–17, 120–21, 135–36, 137
  voice, 88, 103
Lombardi, Vincent (career)
  awards, honors, and record, 7, 177–78
  championships, 6, 7, 44, 49, 74, 80, 129–30, 155, 160
  drilling, 99
  film and video analysis, 39, 93–94
  Fordham University, 4, 38, 50
  and the media, 7, 50, 65, 74, 77, 86, 99, 119–20, 129–30, 161, 169

New York Giants, 5–6, 15, 26, 39, 51, 67–68, 85, 87, 109–10, 121–22, 137
St. Cecilia High School (Englewood, NJ), 4, 28, 37–38, 49, 72–73
semipro football, playing, 3
slogans, stories, anecdotes, and clichés, use of, 70
Super Bowl I, 33, 125–26
Super Bowl II, 7, 49–50, 168, 171, 173–74
United States Military Academy at West Point, 4–5, 39, 90–91, 118
Washington Redskins, 7, 15, 23, 57–58, 83, 92, 110, 122, 139, 157, 175
Lombardi, Vincent (career: leadership process), 1, 6–7, 9, 13–14, 44
  building the team, 18–23
  commitment to excellence, 160–71
  the courage to lead, 129–33
  developing a game plan, 32–35
  innovation, imagination, and creativity, 37–42
  inspiration and motivation, 72–78
  keeping things simple, 67–70
  knowledge and expertise, 25–30
  learning, teaching, and practice, 90–96
  love, family, and heart power, 144–51
  physical fitness, discipline, and mental toughness, 98–107, 170
  preparation, 13–16
  the price of success, 153–58
  race, dealing with, 62–65
  running to daylight, 109–14
  self-control, 135–42
  selling self, 47–52
  taking charge, 83–88
  treating people as individuals, 54–60
  will to win, 116–23
Lombardi, Vincent (selected quotations), *xi*
  on building the team, 18
  on building trust, 45
  on commitment to excellence, 160
  on change, 37, 41
  on character, 127
  on creativity, 37
  on defeat, 129, 131
  on developing a game plan, 32
  on drilling the team, 81
  on innovation, 37
  on inspiration and motivation, 72
  on keeping things simple, 67

on leadership, 83
on learning, teaching, and practice, 90
on love, family, and heart power, 144, 147–48, 150–51
on the media, 17
on physical fitness and mental toughness, 98
on preparation, 13
on prejudice, 62
on the price of success, 153
on running to daylight, 109
on self-control, 135
on selling yourself, 47
slogans and maxims, 70, 92–93
on starting out, 11
on treating people as individuals, 54
on winning, 116
Lombardi, Vincent, Jr. (son), 137, 142
Lombardi Award (college football award), 7
Lombardi sweep, 40–41, 166, 167
Lombardi time, 101–2
Lombardi Trophy (NFL Super Bowl award), 7, 178
Long, Bob, 105
Look magazine, 77
Los Angeles Rams, 33, 74, 75, 116, 120, 121, 160
love, 144–51
    Lombardi and, 147–48
    Lombardi on, 144, 147–48, 150–51

MacArthur, Douglas, 118
McClinton, Curtis, 125
McDonald, Ray, 85
McDonald, Tommy, 44
McGee, Max
    breaking the rules, 101, 140
    Lombardi on, 55
    and Lombardi as coach, 23, 58, 59, 91, 92
    Lombardi confiding in, 84–85
    on Lombardi and mistakes, 106
    and Lombardi's temper, 138
    as player, 44
    Super Bowl I, 125
McHan, Lamar, 20, 25, 33, 57
Madden, John, 26
Manuche, Mike, 58
Mara, Wellington, 5, 14, 69
media, Lombardi on, 17
mental toughness, 98–107
    Lombardi on, 98

Mercein, Chuck, 28, 106, 119
    1967 NFL championship game, 162, 165, 166, 167, 168
    visiting Lombardi in the hospital, 176
Meredith, Don
    1967 NFL championship game, 163, 164, 168
Miller, Tom, 91, 119, 133, 140, 146
Minnesota Vikings, 74
Moore, Jerry, 105
Moore, Father Timothy, 38, 177
motivation, 72–78
    Lombardi on, 72

National Football League (NFL)
    1958 NFL championship game, 121–22
    1962 NFL championship game, 123
    1966 NFL championship game, 125
    1967 NFL championship game, 160–68
    and racial equality, 62–63
Nellen, James, 161
New Orleans Saints, 144–45
New York Giants, 5–6, 7, 15, 26, 39, 51, 67–68, 80, 85, 87, 109–10, 120
    1958 NFL championship game, 121–22
    1962 NFL championship game, 123
    Eddie Price incident, 137
New York Post, 99, 129
New York Sports, 65
New York Times, 129
New York University, 32
Newsweek magazine, 130
Nitschke, Ray, 107
    and the Berlin Crisis call-up, 120
    and criticism, 59
    drinking at bar incident, 135–36
    Lombardi on, 60
    on Lombardi, 178
    on Lombardi as coach, 157
    on Lombardi's soft heart, 150
    Lombardi's verbal abuse of, 54–55, 104
    1967 NFL championship game, 165
    as player, 20, 22, 34
    on running to win, 121

Oakland Raiders
    Super Bowl II, 7, 49–50, 168, 171, 173–74
I Corinthians, vii

Paquin, Leo, 64
Paul, St., *vii*
Peppler, Pat, 111–12, 113, 146
Philadelphia Eagles, 32, 44, 49, 86, 156
physical fitness, 98–107
　Lombardi on, 98
Pitts, Elijah, 106, 126
Pittsburgh Steelers, 28
Power Sweep, 40–41, 166, 167
practice, 90–96
　Lombardi on, 90
prejudice, dealing with, 62–65
　Lombardi on, 62
preparation, 13–16
　Lombardi on, 13
price of success, Lombardi on, 153
Price, Eddie, 137
Promuto, Vince, 100, 110
　on Lombardi, 179
Pugh, Jethro
　1967 NFL championship game, 164,
　　167, 168, 169

Quinlan, Bill, 19, 21

race, dealing with, 62–65
　Lombardi on, 62
racial equality and professional football,
　62–65
redshirting, 40
Reeves, Dan, 164
Rentzel, Lance, 164
Ringo, Jim, 34, 86, 106, 112–13
Robinson, Dave, 103
Rockne, Knute, 2, 13
Rollow, Cooper, 105
Rondou, Father David, 170
Rooney, Art, 28
Rote, Kyle, 6, 85
Rozelle, Pete, 125, 170, 178
running to daylight, 109–14
　Lombardi on, 109

St. Cecilia High School (Englewood,
　NJ), 4, 28, 37–38, 49, 72–73
St. Francis Prep School (Brooklyn), 2
St. Louis Cardinals, 76
　and racism, 63
Saturday Evening Post, 50
Schnelker, Bob, 111
Schoenke, Ray, 85, 141
Scott, Ray, 169
self-control, 135–42
　Lombardi on, 135

selling self, 47–52
　Lombardi on, 47
Shaugnessey, Clark, 38
Shofner, Dale, 80
simple, keeping things, 67–70
　Lombardi on, 67
single-wing offense, 38
Skoronski, Bob, 44, 55, 76, 107, 117,
　125
　1967 NFL championship game, 165,
　　166, 168
　visiting Lombardi in the hospital, 176
Slattery, Dave, 76
slogans and maxims, 70, 92–93
Smith, Jerry, 178
Smith, Red, 123
Sport's Illustrated, 7
Starr, Bart, 57
　Lombardi on, 55, 56
　on Lombardi, 179, 180
　on Lombardi as coach, 35, 47, 48,
　　56–57, 84, 117, 121, 171
　on Lombardi as an influence, 107
　and the Lombardi sweep, 40–41, 166,
　　167
　and Lombardi time, 101
　on Lombardi and winning, 122
　on Lombardi's Catholicism, 139–40
　on Lombardi's enthusiasm, 49
　and Lombardi's motivational impact,
　　117
　on Lombardi's slogans, 70
　and Lombardi's temper, 135, 138
　1967 NFL championship game, 162,
　　162–63, 164, 165–68, 171
　as player, 20, 33, 80, 146
　on players cheating in practice, 85
　playing with injuries, 106
　on preparation, 95
　Super Bowl I, 125
　Super Bowl II, 173
　visiting Lombardi in the hospital,
　　176
starting out, Lombardi on, 11
Stram, Hank, 125
Stroud, Jack, 112
success, the price of, 153–58
　Lombardi on, 153
Sumerall, Pat, 26
Super Bowl I, 33, 125–26
Super Bowl II, 7, 49–50, 168, 171,
　173–74
Super Bowl VI, 178
Sutherland, Jock, 40

T formation, 38
taking charge, 83–88
Taylor, Jim
    Lombardi on, 56
    on Lombardi as coach, 158
    on Lombardi's system, 69
    and Lombardi's temper, 138
    media and, 50
    as player, 44, 110, 112
    and team unity, 150
teaching, 90–96
    Lombardi on, 90
team building , 18–23
    Lombardi on, 18
teamwork, 22–23
Thurston, Fred (Fuzzy), 155
    on Lombardi's enthusiasm, 91
    on Lombardi's organization, 25
    and Lombardi's personality, 87
    and Lombardi's temper, 76, 139, 141
    as player, 20, 110
    visiting Lombardi in the hospital, 176
Time magazine, 130
Tittle, Y. A., 80
Townes, Willie
    1967 NFL championship game, 163, 166
treating people as individuals
    Lombardi on, 54
Triplett, Mel, 58
Tunnell, Emlen
    on Green Bay and race, 63–64
    on Lombardi apologizing, 140–41

on Lombardi as coach, 69, 103, 178
on Lombardi as example, 160, 169
on Lombardi's personality, 51
on Lombardi's kindness, 150
as player, 20, 21

Unitas, Johnny, 6
United States Military Academy at West Point, 4–5, 39, 90–91, 118

Van Brocklin, Norm, 44
Villaneuva, Danny, 163

Washington Redskins, 7, 15, 23, 57–58, 63, 83, 92, 110, 122, 139, 157, 175
Whittenton, Jesse, 20
will to win, and leadership, 116–23
Williams, Edward Bennett, 65, 76, 83, 175
Williams, Travis
    1967 NFL championship game, 162
Wilson, Ben, 29
    1967 NFL championship game, 162
winning, Lombardi on, 116
Wood, Willie, 20, 21, 22, 75, 126
    1967 NFL championship game, 161
    visiting Lombardi in the hospital, 176
Wright, Steve, 138